YOU
EVOLUTIONARY CODE
UNLEASHED

Your Magical Evolutionary Code Unleashed

YOUR MAGICAL EVOLUTIONARY CODE UNLEASHED

THE SCIENCE OF INNER RESONANCE

Maureen Edwardson

First Published in Canada 2011 by Influence Publishing

Author's Photo: Cher Bloom
Cover Design: Joe Gregory

About the Author

Maureen developed Inner Resonance Technologies over the last twenty years traveling internationally, sharing with the Russian doctors of the Medical Research Institutes in Siberia, the traditional shamans of the Republic of Altai, and healing centres in Norway and Sweden. She also provided training over a three-year period to Tribal Schools for the Office of Indian Education Programs, Bureau of Indian Affairs, United States Government. Maureen worked privately with and also provided training for all stake holders in the educational process including children, parents, teachers, TA's, Special Education, counsellors, administrators, bus drivers and cafeteria staff. Most children involved became self-managed eliminating their need for Ritalin.

Maureen has also worked extensively in helping people clear the underlying painful causes to addictive substance abuse and patterns, freeing and empowering people to make new, healthier choices.

Maureen delivers her sessions by phone or in person, individually or in groups, and teaches her concepts in workshops for personal transformation and for other health practitioners wanting to have a catalyst for even more effective results.

Her Resonance Bodywork integrates her advanced techniques to empower clients to reprogram for optimal health with tools for ongoing self-care.

Maureen's favourite thing is to give live presentations and to pass on the concepts of our potential through freeing up our magical selves.

She has proudly helped produce two amazing daughters, both engaged in their passion for life, one working with horses, the other a musician.

Maureen lives on beautiful Bowen Island off the coast of Vancouver, Canada where she enjoys the forest and the ocean when she finds herself at home.

To contact Maureen for information regarding private sessions, workshops, or to book her as an Inspirational Speaker, please go to her website.
www.innerresonance.com or email her at
maureen@innerresonance.com

Praise

"Maureen Edwardson is not only my author, but a dear friend I feel honoured to know. Wouldn't we all want a friend like Maureen, whose Inner Resonance work can give you INSTANT results to those niggling, frustrating things that stop you from moving forward? Wouldn't it be great if you had a friend you could call when challenged.....and then start to see results the moment you put the phone down?" Well Maureen is one of those people. Frustrated people owe you money and not answering your emails? One call to Maureen and the outstanding monies start magically appearing in your inbox! Niggled by a constant body pain that just won't leave you alone? One call to Maureen and you can feel instant relief! Is this really possible? Yes it is and the Magical Evolutionary Code is now available to you, packaged in a book! You will learn how to tap into the code of Inner Resonance and change your belief patterns that are holding you back, effortlessly!"
Julie Salisbury, Influence Publishing

"I had never felt completely whole, but this process has allowed me to become ME, a total human being: Spirit, mind, and body."
Carla M. Taos, New Mexico.

"Thank you for giving me back my life."
Donna K. Oregon

"I have no more arthritis pain!"
Darlene, Chilliwack after one session.

"I have never felt so free and so joyful! My asthma is completely gone!! And I didn't have to believe. In fact this relief happened in spite of my scepticism".
Fran Hewitt, Langley BC., after a group demo and follow up private session.

"Maureen Edwardson has done several years of healing alternative therapy work at the Quileute Tribal School at La Push, Washington. She worked periodically from January 1996 through April 1998. During this time she worked with community members, students, and staff. Ms. Edwardson's work successfully reached those who were not successful with the traditional client and mental health therapists' model. Our community has suffered a lot of intergenerational crises and trauma. It has affected all ages emotionally, spiritually, physically, and intellectually. Maureen's unique methods of quickly being able to bring pattern interruptions to long term dysfunctional behaviour has been documented and successful for many members in the La Push Community and at the Quileute Tribal School.

She was asked to represent the Quileute Tribal School at the National Indian School Board Conference. An Exceptional Education Grant was later funded to share her work among several Native American Communities through the Bureau of Indian Affairs organization. Maureen has made her method available by sharing her knowledge to our staff in various training and workshops.

I would not hesitate to highly recommend her services. She is always professional in nature, and has a very fine personal integrity as well. She truly has a wonderful spirit. Some of our most challenged students have met real sustained growth and success on the road to healing with her sessions. She always has included the family members in her approach. Her follow up care is also admirable."
Franklin S. Hanson, Superintendent QTS

"I approached this class with scepticism. It's true that I believed in the possibility of emotional and physical healing through suggestion. Also, I have successfully used the 'power of positive thought'. However, the idea of being able to teach a person to help heal themselves was daunting. Not because of the skill involved, but because it is outside of what I considered 'normal'.

The course covered four intensive days. There were six students and two instructors. We listened, talked, shared and finally facilitated healing. I volunteered as one of the first clients, because I didn't think I could remember all of the questions I needed to ask as a facilitator, even though the sheets were provided.

I know the student who facilitated my healing had many questions and doubts about this process. I was sceptical, but trying to stay open to the possibility. In spite of these doubts, healing took place. I was impressed.

I still had questions though. I wondered if I could really do this on my own. I wanted to know how the technique could be used with the students in exceptional education. I kept asking questions with different students in mind, trying to imagine how I could work with each of them. I practiced facilitation with my classmates. The class ended too soon.

The next day one of my students came into the resource room tense, angry and unwilling to work. After five minutes of 'Mind Body Magic' techniques, he went to work, willing and cheerfully. The next day another student came into class and began to cause trouble. After talking to him, I discovered he had a new set of problems at home. We were able to set those aside, using more of the techniques I learned in the Mind Body Magic class, so that he could complete the day without getting in trouble.

My third experiment as a facilitator was with my husband. He too, was sceptical, but willing to humour me. He asked me to get rid of the constant arthritis pain in his knee and wrists. I didn't believe I could, but I went through the session anyway, for practice.

That was only four days ago. However, a change of weather will usually cause his arthritis symptoms to flare, and although there have been several major shifts in the weather in the last four days, he is free of pain. Hard physical work will also increase his symptomology. Except this time, his full day digging in the new garden two days ago only resulted in sore muscles. I'm not yet willing to say that his arthritis is cured. He has been free of pain for four days. That's a fact.

I am still not sure how to describe the Mind Body Magic. I cannot say how or why the physical or emotional healing takes place. But it does. I am still sceptical, but not as sceptical. Through this class, I discovered non-invasive techniques for empowering students. I discovered I could help others heal themselves. I cannot explain how this works, and I am not comfortable telling everyone that I am facilitating healing, because it is not accepted as 'normal'. But it works."

Evelyn Satterlee, Head of Special Education, Quileute Tribal School

"I am hoping this letter finds you in a good way and provides for you similar good feelings to the ones I encounter when I reflect on this point.

I remember the "Resonance Healing" Training that I undertook. Some time has passed. Close to five years I think; but, it is like it happened last week.

Something special happened for me in that training. You will recall that I wanted to give over the pain that I harbored in my arms. Modern medical doctors likened it to "tendonitis" and / or "tennis elbow". I had acquired the pain in a car accident nearly fifteen years before our training session. Obviously, I had become quite accustomed to carrying that pain. The pain had precluded me from many things I loved, crocheting, needlepoint and beadwork. I also experienced bouts of pain that made it difficult for me to work on the computer at work (at that time computer work was just becoming a necessity in my work). I had given up hope of ever being "cured" or of having freedom from this pain.

Then, resonance healing changed all that for me. I remember clearly the exercise and I remember my eyes were closed and others in the training were watching. The trainee I was working with had declared herself a skeptic, but she lifted that pain from my arms and I remember the feeling that I had as I 'gave over' the pain.

Today I can only tell you the pain has never returned. I am able to use the computer at work and I do beadwork and crochet, when I have time. I have to tell you that I am grateful for you and for the unselfish way that you share your gift. Thank you."
Shirley Hardman, Coordinator Aboriginal Programs,
University of the Fraser Valley, Chilliwack, BC.

"The two days we spent together were an opening for me – to a new way of working. I appreciated the opportunity to connect with people I didn't know before – and with the guests who came in. I do look forward to trying this healing tool with the people I work with. My interest in the way that the human organism works in all its parts, and as a unit, has been kindled – or re-kindled – or kindled in a new way."
Patricia, Health Program Coordinator, Maximum Security
Prison.

"I am so thankful for this time in learning the tools to help others help themselves. I have always wanted to help people who are hurting and in pain, but counselling didn't really appeal to me. It seemed too long and painful a situation. When I would 'counsel' others I would feel like I had so much power, and that it was up to me to show this person 'the way'… how totally un-empowering for the other person, and too much pressure for myself. Helping others isn't about power.

In the sense of controlling others, it's about gaining power over our selves. I've heard stories of mind over matter healing and I always wondered 'how' does it work? Now I have some tools to allow it to happen."
Yalh yexw kw'as hoy!
Helena

Dedication

For all those who are tired of being buried in old programs that cover and smother their creative selves;

For those that are awake to our collective crises and who are ready to work together to find solutions;

For those who know they have a role to play but can't quite see it or feel it yet;

For those that know their role but can't activate it;

For those that are activated but are feeling impatient;

For those who know, deep down in their core that we are not designed for struggle but for joy;

For those that see the light but don't know how to reach it.

For all those lost souls who are looking to find themselves and in that finding, lose themselves in their passion for making a difference in a purpose so much bigger than themselves;

For those who are found and want to take the next steps; and for all those that know we must step together, because we each are part of the whole and the whole cannot be complete without our shared unique gifts.

This book is dedicated to you and your higher self that knows clearly who you are.

Contents

Acknowledgements

I have always been envious reading other books to see what a lot of community of support it takes to get a book birthed into the world. I have felt very alone in those times, probably because I was not ready to get my book "out there". Now that it is time, the right and most amazing community have shown up for full backing of this project. Julie Salisbury of Influence Publishing and Inspire A Book is our guide, dedicated to do everything it takes to birth our messages into the world in the most successful way. Like a mother struggling and sometimes fighting to give birth, it is not always a pretty picture being a Book Doula. As fledgling authors we are struggling to get our unique messages into the greater world. I have experienced full on capacity of our publisher and our collective co-creative community to evolve a new paradigm of publishing that is nothing short of miraculous. It has been, and continues to be, an amazing moveable feast of constant adaptation and evolving forms to be the best possible. We are all learning together. The favourite line: "Oh...that was LAST week". Co-Creation is not for the faint of heart but the next way forward if we are to survive and be sustainable as a species; and as we find our way to have our own way that blends with everyone else's own way, that still supports our unique voices, this is magic indeed. Our collaborative co-creative community of authors are so gifted and generous spirited, un-burying their heads to respond to feedback or ideas in the throes of their own deadlines or creative splurges. Everyone shows up, open hearted, dedicated to everyone's success. That is the power of this collective model.

So I say thank you to all of you….you know who you are….that have stood by me even when you may not have agreed with or understood what my book is about. That is the added blessing, as we are so diverse in our inspired messages and yet can fully support each other's projects. Yes, I am grateful.

Thank you to all my students and clients who, through my open curiosity to ask the right questions, have not only given surprising answers but provided new questions to evolve this process further, just when I thought it was complete. Of course now I know it could never be complete, just like the rest of creation which is always expanding and evolving.

My gratitude to those who, having responded from within to demonstrate the amazing life transformations that show our human capacity for miracles, have given me the inspiration from their successes and the strength to build on my failures in order to refine Inner Resonance Technologies into what it continues to be today.

The results are in these pages. There is much more to share than I could put into this first book; however the simple basics are required as a foundation of what is yet to come. With the simplicity being built on so much complexity, the challenge is to navigate the information in balance with processes that address the heart. The heart has the key to unlock our unique code of evolutionary magical potential; unleashing our true birthright as spiritual beings fully integrated with our physical selves, co-commanding and co-evolving our realities. This is what I believe we have been born at this time to experience: The passion of our evolutionary potential unleashed, in service to each other, as we explore further together than one person alone ever could.

I am also thankful for those of my friends, students and clients who have encouraged me, even bullied me for many years to get this work into the larger world and given me valuable feedback when my sight was veiled or my brain overwhelmed and resistant. I too am a work in progress. I am thankful to my own Self for showing up even when I felt like a failure, continuously saying YES to life with an irrepressible optimism that seems to be my signature.

I am especially grateful and humble to be standing on the shoulders of some very great people, currently involved in continuously cutting the edge of our scientific understandings of consciousness and the spirit/mind/body potential. These pioneers both ancient and modern have created a scaffold on which to climb to an expanded view of reality and build on our evolutionary possibilities…a most exciting time to be alive and part of the moving edge.

Thanks from the bottom of my heart to the limitless heights of my Spirit!

"It's in every one of us,
to be wise,

Find your heart,
Open up both your eyes,

We can all know everything,
without ever knowing why,

It's in every one of us,
By and by."

Lyrics to song by David Pomeranz

*"The value of knowing that it can be done by me;
Just knowing it was inside me and what it can be used
for."*

Amelia, Inner Resonance student, South Dakota

Introduction: Who Are We: Really?

The nature of our Universe is expansion. We are constantly in a state of evolution. Mostly this happens by default, leaving us feeling like victims of everything that seems outside of ourselves. This worldview is at the edge of disintegration, being against the higher laws of nature.

Dr. Bruce Lipton points out that, like our body which appears to be one organism but instead is really a community of cells, we are, each of us, a cell in the greater body of creation. This gives meaning and understanding to spiritual quotes including this one from the Bible that teaches "What you do to the least of these you do to yourself". There is no separation. As the scientist David Suzuki says, we are breathing in particles of recycled atmosphere that has the memory of all life from the beginning of time. Physically, we are ONE from the perspective of this miniature world. Therefore part of who we are, is recycled. If we are truly made of the stuff of the universe, if we are a cell in the body of creation and creation itself is expanding, so must we be, as an integral part of that system.

With new bridges being built between those old antagonists, Science and Spirit, a wondrous new land is being opened up for exploration and creation of expanded possibilities. We are adventuring to a new place of quantum squatting, staking out our individual claims only to find out that we can only build this new world together. Each of our gifts represents a brick, a piece of the multidimensional puzzle that, only by putting our unique selves together, will be whole. A place with new laws is being discovered with a strange way to live – one that, surprising to some, is in total balance and harmony with natural and universal laws. A land of ancient

1

opportunities indeed: An interactive world with each of us having our own command centre within to co-create in harmony with all that is in our visible and invisible universe - a place of magical evolution. However, this appears to be a gated community! What is the key for entry? How do we find this magical evolutionary access code?

We can only come to this new paradigm by shedding our clothing of past beliefs and limiting programs, coming to our fresh creation naked as the day we were banged from singularity, pure as Source Itself. What? A nudist colony you might ask? Remember the spiritual clothing of compassion, love, understanding and respect for all of life? These are part of the empowered co-creators' new wardrobe.

To enter, one must know the code within, the ME code, the Magical Evolutionary Code that is the centre of our individual universe. As the character Polonius said in the Shakespearean play Hamlet, "Know thyself, and to thine own self be true": Herein lays humanity's heroic quest.

Inner Resonance is a key to unlocking your authentic self. It is in this clarity of our uniqueness that we are connected to the vast oneness of the collective consciousness with all the potential of the quantum field with which to dance and consciously co-create and birth new realities, more sustainable than the one we are currently destroying.

Who are we, really? This book is designed to help you uncover and discover that, to facilitate you to self-clear the way to your core, creative, miraculous and authentic self. We can then fully participate in the great SHIFT of the ages, predicted long ago, to evolve ourselves and our world to the next level of expression. Relax. Let go. There is nothing to do but everything to be and allow. The Truth is so simple and often counter-intuitive. As one client expressed it recently:

"And the further insight that came to me while on the patio right now was this...just like once we issue a command to our computer we would do best to just sit back and wait for the website or whatever to come up. If we relax/receive and do the same once we have Inner Resonance commands set into motion, things just work out a whole lot better than sitting there punching buttons and sending overload commands to our body's innate healing mechanisms!

Once the commands are in motion, our only job is to relax, receive, and act upon awareness as inner guided. That's it, plain and simple."

Angela, California.

By clearing all that we are not, our Magical Evolutionary Code is automatically unleashed and we are attracted forward to all our greater good with effortless grace. After all, we are spiritual beings co-creating and birthing our evolved selves and our world through the science of miracles. Let's do it consciously and together! It will be a lot more fun!

Chapter 1: Invitation to the Journey

I am delighted to welcome you to this adventure of consciousness! Together we can explore beyond the frontiers of mind/body to the limitless Human Spirit, creating new possibilities and realities, beyond our current limited beliefs.

"Someone asked us recently, 'Is there any limitation to the body's ability to heal?' And we said, 'None other than the belief that you hold.' And he said, 'Then why aren't people growing new limbs?' And we said, 'Because no one believes that they can',"

Abraham Hicks.

Interestingly, many years ago in my talks I would share that when a young child has an injury that severs part of or a whole digit from their hand or foot, most often their bodies re-grow a fully functional part. This also goes for a thumb, for example that has been torn off and is stitched back on for "cosmetic effect." Almost always I would get stories from the audience of first or second hand accounts of this happening. The child has not learned from his environment that this is impossible, so the body is free to regenerate itself from the energetic blueprint.

Einstein is quoted as saying that we can't solve a problem with the same consciousness that created it. Goodness knows we need new and different solutions for our troubled times. Indeed we need a paradigm shift: a shift in perception of who we really are.

Over the last 20 years I have been on a journey of discovery resulting in an amazing technique I am excited to share with you called Inner Resonance Technologies (IRT).

Why amazing?

- IRT allows you to create immediate, permanent change in 1-4 sessions in ALL areas of our lives
- IRT does not require you to relive or re-experience or understand anything to put this inner technology to work for yourself.
- IRT works as a catalyst to boost every system, process and technique into the instant results of quantum timelessness.
- IRT gives you the opportunity to program a one-touch 'speed dial' for ongoing maintenance and activation

Truly, we are walking miracles, born 'fully loaded' with all the programs our 'bio-supercomputers' need to instantly heal our bodies, clear our minds and reconnect our spirits, allowing us to feel whole once again.

Pauline O'Malley of "The Revenue Builder" has referred to IRT as 'the Windows of the bio- computer system' as what I have created is a unique breakthrough:

An extremely user-friendly interface between the operator (conscious 5%) and the operating system (unconscious 95%) resulting in everyday miracles: the automatic outcome of clearing old limiting patterns and beliefs.

The Body as Super-Computer Technology

The Body is an incredible piece of technology, a Magical Machine.

The body is often thought of as our human limitation. The truth is that it is capable of 'miracles'. If we were to take the entire DNA in our bodies and stretch it out, it would encircle the globe 5,000 times! Each molecule of DNA is such a powerful processor that it has been used to run a nano-computer the size of a drop of water, no external power source needed. This was shared in Scientific American in 2003. We have 50 to 100 trillion cells in our bodies. According to Jon Kabat Zinn, a Western Zen monk, the liver handles 100,000 enzymatic processes every second. The brain processes 40 neural bits per second at the conscious level, 40 million bits per second at the unconscious, and the non-local mind of super-consciousness is instant.

This is indeed the power needed for miracles. What is a miracle except something that occurs beyond our capacity to explain or understand it?

"Any sufficiently advanced technology is indistinguishable from magic."

Arthur C. Clark, the author of "2001 A Space Odyssey"

Electricity is like magic when you have never seen it before, and we can only imagine remote tribes seeing an airplane for the first time. What we don't understand is classified as miraculous.

New Science, like Dr. Bruce Lipton's "Biology of Belief", of how DNA responds to the environment which includes our thoughts and emotions, is gaining ground into mainstream understandings.

The body is a responder to consciousness, which is limitless in its nature. Bruce shows us the mechanisms of how consciousness changes DNA, so we are not victims even to our genetic inheritance. With this new awareness comes empowerment as the co-creators we already are, to consciously and proactively interact and resonate with that greater field of information often referred to as the Quantum Field, Divine Matrix or the Vacuum.

Physicists Nassim Haramein and Hal Puthoff (www.theresonanceproject.org) refer to the Vacuum or Zero Point Field as a place of infinite potential from which all our future power could be sourced. In The New Scientist magazine in 2009 it was postulated that the body is such a source of energy, being a superconductor at room temperature, that in future instead of needing surgery to replace the batteries for a pacemaker every 10 years, we might just call on the body's own energy reserves to recharge those same batteries. The article also mentioned the possibility of having a body patch to charge up our cell phones and other devices. Talk about cheap renewable resources! Everything is within us. Recently I was attending my daughter's college graduation. I had forgotten to recharge the batteries for my camera. I filmed the colourful procession of the faculty, but just before it came time for my daughter's unrepeatable walk across the stage for her recognition, my batteries died. Horrors! I took out those batteries and held them against the pride pulsing in my heart. Just as it was her turn, I popped the batteries back into the camera and shot the whole scene with the power required!

These are exciting times as we evolve our understandings of who we really are and put our super bio-computers into full expression of all the magnificence we carry within. Our inner technologies can be fully unleashed instead of using this magic machine for word processing at its lowest level of capacity. That results in having to depend on everything outside ourselves. There is true empowerment available to each of us right now. What I have developed with Inner Resonance Technologies is an elegant interface between the conscious 5% and the 95% subconscious, activating and clearing the way and allowing our super-consciousness full integration to facilitate the transformation of ourselves and our world.

Remember that old saying, "Whatever you can dream you can achieve?"

Inner Resonance Technologies allows us to remember who we are as holographic particles in the greater body of creation in order to consciously create the kind of world, both personal and collective that we have up to this point in our history only dreamed is possible!

What we will do together here in these pages is explore some of the science of co-creation and empowerment, and then share a formula, a quantum key, for putting these concepts to work in the most miraculous ways that not only will uncover our deepest hearts' desires and gifts, but also show how this automatically re-connects us to our greatest collective service. This results in evolving all life into new expressions of inner and outer peace and sustainability for all creation.

This information reveals to you your unique and personal Magical Evolutionary code, putting you on an accelerated journey of purpose and wholeness with the greatest joy and fulfillment beyond what we can imagine from where we sit now. We are on the edge of either destruction or the greatest potential ever realized. Let us unleash the power of our M.E. Code, and evolve ourselves and our universe according to our greatest buried potential and purpose. Let us give birth to our magical selves together though Inner Resonance!

"In that sense, it's truly a birth experience - the ultimate birthing experience of resonance, oneness where the illusion of separation dissolves and where we field the gifts from each of us as a living member of the living planetary body, which we are. I am feeling a joy, an awakening, an opening of our collective eyes and feeling the light that is within every one of us that mystics have experienced. I am feeling that light radiating from us outward into the universe. And I am experiencing the light beyond us of intelligence coming toward us when we resonate and our brainwave patterns synchronize enough to signal to the universe that we are born."

Barbara Marx Hubbard Mar 22, 2011

Chapter 2: Resonance: What is It?

Resonance: A relationship of mutual understanding or trust and agreement between people. Internet.

Electrical Resonance: Zero Resistance in an electrical circuit allows maximum flow of energy. Webster.

Chemical Resonance: Mirrored Balance. Webster

Musical Resonance: Two similar sound wave frequencies meet to create amplification. Webster.

I like to give the example of a stringed instrument, two guitars in fact. One is leaning against the wall by itself; another is being played by a person who plucks the A string. The sound waves resonate and ripple out and hit the whole instrument, but only that second guitar's A string is the same frequency as the one making the sound. As the lonely instrument is activated, it is brought to life through resonance, and its previously silent A string hums along, perfectly in tune with its environment.

Resonance Potential: The energy in volts required to move an electron from a normal orbit to the next nearest orbit. Webster

Everything is energy and everything is within us. So how do we access this inner potential and put it to work for ourselves and our greater lives? The movie "The Secret" went a long way to wake up people to their inner potential. Having an expanded understanding of resonance is a foundation to being and having everything we could dream of. Shakti Gawain, author of "Creative Visualization" said many years ago that we have it all backwards in our society. We want to have everything to be able to do what we want in order to be happy. The reverse is actually the unexpressed key to "The Secret" of life. As we BE who we are, we are then happy and inspired to action which ultimately brings us all of everything we could ever need and desire. So instead of having, doing, being, it is really being, doing, having that runs our lives. No wonder we feel like we are 'hampstering' frantically to nowhere; we are running around in circles... backwards!

There is nothing to do and by just being who we are, in a field clear of old programs and limited beliefs, we are guided moment to moment to more joyful expansion and fulfillment than we can ever imagine. As you rest in the presence of who you are, gifts arrive.

Resonance is the key. When we are in harmony with our essential self, the Self that knows how to be happy for no reason, then we are resonating with our greater good which then arrives effortlessly as if by magic. You see, our higher good is already known within and as we clear the static of fear and old programs that block us, then we can be inspired through our heart based desires to co-create what we really want. The phone rings with an offer, books you need fall off the shelf or open up to exactly the right page, your relationships harmonize spontaneously, money starts to flow, and you realize that you have allowed all this to happen just by focussing on feeling good. Yes, that truly is your main job: To feel good. I love Wayne Dyer's definition of good: Good is God with an extra O. In his work "The Power of Intention", we are encouraged to scrape off the rust on our line to Source in order to have clear connection to and resonance with that greater field of possibilities.

So how do we feel good when we don't feel good? That is a challenge when we lose our job and don't know where our survival is coming from, or have a loved one pass away, or contract a sickness or serious dis-ease. If we can begin to look at life situations as opportunities to grow and re-member the truth of our spiritual selves, then we attract the support we need to clear the underlying causes that keep us stuck in chronic patterns that do not serve us. Life has the whole spectrum of experiences. It is up to us to command the balance and have the perspective that uses every situation to improve and evolve ourselves. This happens best when you do nothing at all, allowing all things. This is where inspiration of right action arises. This is what Inner Resonance facilitates.

The principles of Inner Resonance Technologies show up everywhere and include effortless grace, willingness to be open, and commitment to your journey of evolution. These quotes below echo the words that I teach, in very eloquent ways. It is important to start to notice the information that is available to us in the repeating patterns from the same source of our oneness in a variety of forms. This confirms our own inner knowingness and affirms life.

Effortless Grace

"Grace exists inside of all of us and around us. It is our inner beauty that radiates outward, touching everyone we meet. It is that unseen hand that comes from the divine, raising us up when we most need it. To be able to live in a state of grace is not based on worthiness, nor is it earned through good deeds, ritual, or sacrifice. Rather it is an unearned favour, freely bestowed and available to all, that is inherent to our birthright. All

we must do is open our eyes to its presence and we will find and experience grace everywhere.

www.DailyOm.com May 23, 2011

Opening to Willingness

"Opening ourselves to willingness may feel like we are surrendering or abandoning all that we believed. But at the same time it is an act of power and courage because it is a conscious choice we make about how to apply our personal will. Being willing is to be in a state of willing something into creation. It is at once allowing ourselves to be, while also choosing to direct our energy in a focused way. It is being and doing from a place of openness, where we can work with the universe rather than resist it. It is an open hand rather than one that is clenched into a fist. When we make a step toward willingness, we open ourselves to truth, possibility, and the movement of the wise universe in and through our lives."

www.DailyOm.com Jan 21, 2008

The Resonance of Commitment

"Until one is committed there is hesitancy, the chance to draw back, always ineffectiveness.

Concerning all acts of initiative and creation, there is one elementary truth, the ignorance of which kills countless ideas and splendid plans: that the moment one definitely commits oneself then providence moves too.

All sorts of things occur to help one that would never otherwise have occurred. A whole stream of events issues from the decision, raising in one's favour all manner of unforeseen incidents, meetings and material assistance which no man could have dreamt would come his way. Whatever you can do or dream you can… Begin it. Boldness has genius, power and magic in it."

Johann Wolfgang Von Goethe

Chapter 3: My Journey: I Just Happened to Be There

I laughingly tell people that my middle name is "I Just Happened to Be There!" Some would call it Divine Stupidity!!! I didn't know what was "impossible".

I guess it is the gift of true ignorance called not knowing: open-mindedness or beginner's mind.

Ever since my childhood growing up in a fundamentalist environment, I was the bane of the adults in my world, always asking the "why" questions long after my three year old phase should have settled.

Inner Resonance Technologies has evolved out of my own personal journey of healing, as is often the case with new discoveries. The death of my mother before my first daughter was a year old put me on a spiritual quest that was the foundation for much of what followed.

When my children were very young, I found myself in a steadily deteriorating relationship, and so I went for psychiatric help, as I felt that I couldn't resolve my situation alone. With that help and with my developing spiritual understanding, I did my best to use the situation to make myself better: a crucible if you will! (I am certain that my "ex" has a completely different view of this time!!)

A childhood trauma of mine was triggered when my girls were 4 and 6, and so my search for healing was intensified, knowing that it must affect every part of me in ways that I could never fully understand consciously. I went back to my psychiatrist who was not able to help me, but referred me to hands on healers, a very wise man!

I threw myself headlong into a variety of workshops and techniques where everyone around me was processing their old pain, apparently successfully- except me! I was even a failure at getting better it seemed! The 'better' I was becoming, the worse my marriage seemed to get, and so the inevitable life of the single mother became a reality the year my children turned 8 and 10.

Before the 23 year marriage ended I had been drawn to take training with a man named Roger La Chance whose work changed names over the years from the Unicorn Method to Release Work and finally, The La Chance Method. I was the first practitioner to bring Roger's work to Canada and I certified over a hundred and thirty people in his method as practitioners and teachers. I also served on the Board of Directors of his newly formed International Release Worker's Association.

However, as my own experience and knowledge grew, that organization could not contain my inquiring, independent creativity. I realized finally that it was time for me to take responsibility for my own gifts which were rapidly unfolding and to start teaching and sharing my own discoveries. I discovered that I had the gift of 'ignorance'. Because of not having formal training in any scientific or medical fields, I was free to ask questions that many others were too conditioned to ask as the answers were already 'known' and accepted as reality in the paradigm of that time.

The answers that I was getting in my 'labs' of private sessions and workshops combined to surprise even me in their profundity! I can honestly say that most of what I have learned in this field has been given to me by my clients and students, in process together. When I first started giving workshops, I felt that I should be paying participants for their knowledge instead of the other way around! I was a born collaborator it seems now, looking back on my life.

We fast forward to the spring of 1995. I love road trips. It was on such a journey that, once again, I just happened to be there. Remember my middle name? I also call myself 'Unconsciously Conscious' as I have been invisibly guided to the right place at the right time in spite of myself. This was one of those times.

I had been doing some 'Mind Body Magic' workshops in Crestone, Colorado, one of my homes away from home. It was a beautiful sunny May morning high in the Sangre de Cristo Mountains and I needed a solid breakfast to carry me onto my long journey back to Vancouver Canada. The Road Kill Restaurant was just the ticket! I loved that place, not necessarily the name but the great food and the community flavour. I wandered out into the sun-drenched garden warmth. The place was packed as usual so I plopped myself down beside some folks at a picnic table with a space on the edge. Turns out that to my left were a couple I had heard about but did not get a chance to meet during my stay. They too had been disappointed to have missed me, as he had a bad right elbow that just happened to be beside me, and wanted help. So between ordering and having my amazing breakfast appear, I naturally guided him through my technique. Instant healing happened. We were all impressed, but he especially so that he disappeared momentarily, coming back with freshly copied tapes of Deepak Chopra's "Ageless Body, Timeless Mind". He had brought them with him that morning, not sure who they were for. They quickly found their destiny in my car's tape deck and jet-fuelled my drive home. The journey, needless to say, was one of excited inspiration that gave remarkable foundation to what I had developed and called

"Mind Body Magic". I loved that later the same year Deepak Chopra's new book came out called "Body Mind and Soul – The Mystery and the Magic". We are all accessing the same Source.

Soon after arriving back at my quaint village, Fort Langley, the historic "Birthplace of BC" and also of my children, I was introduced to the work of Dr. Bruce Lipton, a cellular biologist. After his scientific/spiritual epiphany, Bruce was on his own road trips, teaching what he was then calling The Biology of Consciousness which demonstrated how our thoughts and emotions become behaviours in our bodies and our lives. I became an insatiable groupie. I was the inevitable gadfly fluttering frantically front and centre with questions that did not seem to have answers…that is, immediate ones. It turned out that Dr. Lipton, unconsciously to him, became my main research tool at the time. He had access and 'drive' to answer those burning questions and always came back next time with answers and updated information. This continued about four times that year until the answers slowed down, or probably more correctly, the fire of questions died down to a smolder while integration and evolution took place in my world.

Jump forward again 10 years to Lipton's Vancouver book launch of his long awaited "Biology of Belief" the spring of 2005. It seemed like it was always spring when my world took a leap forward. Living on an island, I am of necessity, very early for most events. The Vancouver Planetarium was also hosting an exhibition of the work of Albert Einstein, another of my heroes. I was so absorbed that as I rounded a great concrete column, my physical world collided with that of Bruce's: We literally crashed into each other. What was even more remarkable is that he seemed to remember me! Oh my goodness, had I been that much of a troublemaker? I have always had too many questions it seemed.

In a short while I once again sat entranced front and centre and was amazed that within the missing 10 years I had evolved my work in ways that seemed to also be on Dr. Lipton's current front page. Of course I waited with the mesmerized after-crowd to thank him and briefly share his role as such an important catalyst in the evolution of my own work, now called Inner Resonance Technologies which was a direct application of his cutting edge scientific principles. Two years later, IRT was included in the resources section on his website, and also recently in his latest book "Spontaneous Evolution", co-authored by Steve Bhaerman.

Sitting in the planetarium that day was truly an experience out of this world!

Chapter 4:
Here, There or Everywhere?
Quantum Science Made Easy

This chapter is for those who just want the BONES, the skeletal concepts on which Inner Resonance hangs and of which IRT is the outer, or should I say inner, expression. All the science throughout this chapter, as well as scattered throughout the book are resourced in Appendix 4, so please enjoy the adventure of following your own intrigued curiosity to pursue more of what your heart and mind are pulling you towards. The whole principle of Inner Resonance is simplicity: you need to know nothing, or even share a thing in order to have the magic happen. Your subconscious and super-conscious do all the work for you outside of your field of conscious awareness. You just need to give permission to release all that limits you unnecessarily. Automatically you are then drawn with clarity and inspiration in the right directions for everything else you might want or need. Life is a continuous, upwardly flowing spiral when you are resonating with your greater good and your authentic self.

Therefore, here are some of the scientific principles that have excited me, catalyzed and given substance and understanding to what Inner Resonance Technologies is all about. This part of the book is my personal interpretation and inspiration of possibilities that have sprung from these sources. I beg forgiveness of any one's work or the science here that I may have misinterpreted and invite correction where needed. All here is my limited perception, as after all is said and done I am an inspired layperson.

It's All About Resonance:
Candace Pert's Molecules of Emotional Neuropeptides

Candace Pert's contribution to my understanding was a major shift in my paradigm of the subconscious. She made the parallel that the body is the subconscious mind. That was such an amazing thought and it corresponded to the idea of body memory that most physical therapists, including myself as a body worker, see expressed constantly. This made total sense.

What I also appreciated about Pert's work is that she explained how the neuropeptide chemicals of emotions are linked from the brain to the appropriate receptor, or ligand, by the principle of resonance. This was also an important upgrade for me of the previous image used of lock and key to describe this process. Resonance seemed to be a more organic, feminine principle; that of the law of attraction, not hardware for making something happen. While her contribution was even greater, those were the main ideas that "neoned" into my awareness. For more please read Candace Pert's pioneering book "Molecules of Emotion".

* we are what we believe. And, as we believe so we are.

  We manifest, with each breath we take, the sum total of our miscreations.

* Focusing on "as above so below," we are awaiting God's bringing heaven down to Earth for us. Yet what we're missing is this; what we're witnessing here below is the reflection of what we ~~have~~ have created above!

  Now, we must clear our miss creations in the ethereal so that we create divine oness. That then will reflect downward.

TY# 9 ETHERIC

*2 In "The Violet Flame", what we send out in thought, beliefs and emotions attract (magnetically) like substance and adds to what we send out — on its way back home.

Talk to the Genes:
The Resonant Science of Bruce Lipton's Biology of Belief

I think of Bruce Lipton as the Father of Epigenetics. Epi means above, therefore epigenetics literally means above the genes: it is a signal from the environment (which includes our thoughts and emotions) that causes the expression of the genetic blueprint. Bruce aptly points out that a blueprint is never self-activating but needs interpretation and instructions. One needs a contractor to read the blueprint of a house to have somewhere to live and experience life. It is all so simple and obvious.

Dr. Lipton's New Biology gave me an updated impression of the body being the subconscious mind. It turns out that as the wheel of science grinds, the memories are now shown not to actually be in the body or brain at all, but in a field all around us. I like to refer to that as the mine(d)field (just one shift up the alphabet after all). I gathered from this new understanding that just as the cell has receptors to respond to the environment, the body, by the same model, with the sensory receptors of ears, eyes, nose, mouth, skin is only a much larger community of cells, expressing our thoughts and emotions. So it is perhaps more accurate to say that the body is the mirror of the subconscious mind, reflecting the emotions, thoughts and beliefs of our experience.

Our bodies are nothing more than responders, but instant responders, to the mindfield of greater consciousness and limitless potential. So what's the deal? Why is it such a struggle?

27

The information of past experience, current events, even future fears all resonate in our field to create charged static that blocks and interferes with our ability to connect to our best selves and our creativity, connected into the greater field of potential.

The information in the field is resonating with and activating the body's capacity as a responder and expresser of the environment of our consciousness. This is why we are always being told to listen to our bodies. What are they telling us? Listen to our gut and follow our heart. We will speak more of the heart in a short while.

Dr. Lipton shows us the pathways that thoughts and emotions travel to create behavioural outcome in our bodies and our lives. Every thought and every emotion has a chemical that gets produced in the brain which then sends a signal to the receptors on the cell membrane, linked and attracted through resonance. Bruce Lipton shows how those receptors are activated through our perceptions to the environment. Our subconscious programs act like magnets, attracting similar 'new' experiences that resonate with the body which then acts out our reactions with behaviour that expresses what we are thinking and feeling. This becomes the same old same - old tapes. So it is external signals, magnetically attracted from within our own 'charged' past experience or the stored experience of our ancestors that activate the expression of our genes. Change our environment which includes our thoughts and feelings and we change the behaviour of our bodies as well as our minds, our lives and ultimately our world.

*2

"Until recently, it was thought that genes were self-actualizing...that genes could 'turn themselves on and off.' Such behavior is required in order for genes to control biology. Though the

28

power of genes is still emphasized in current biology courses and textbooks, a radically new understanding has emerged at the leading edge of cell science. It is now recognized that the environment, and more specifically, our perception (interpretation) of the environment, directly controls the activity of our genes. Environment controls gene activity through a process known as epigenetic control. This new perspective of human biology does not view the body as just a mechanical device, but rather incorporates the role of a mind and spirit.

This breakthrough in biology is fundamental in all healing for it recognizes that when we change our perception or beliefs we send totally different messages to our cells and reprogram their expression. The new-biology reveals why people can have spontaneous remissions or recover from injuries deemed to be permanent disabilities."

Dr. Bruce Lipton article "Mind Over Genes

The most exciting news from this understanding that the mind and spirit commands the expression of our DNA is that there are no more victims of our genetic inheritance. Dr. Lipton was awarded the Japanese GOI international peace prize in September 2009 for his contribution to world peace based on this principle. We are responsible, able to respond (indeed are always responding) to the environment through our perceptions in order to change our bodies and our lives. Now that we have awareness of this understanding, we can begin to consciously intend our collective intelligence to clear our field of old experiences that result in erroneous beliefs that keep us dancing to an old tune. This frees us up to make new choices much more resonant with our soul's purpose, as our free hearts can dance passionately in harmony with the music of the spheres….the universal dance of wholeness that activates our magical selves to unleash the evolutionary code of our unique contribution fully expressed as we evolve our collective selves.

Unified Fields of Resonance:
Brilliant Breakthroughs of Nassim Haramein

Once again I just happened to be invited to my friend's house one day to watch some science DVDs. I was overdue for a visit and was curious, so I went over and ended up staying the night to watch another 2 hours the next day of what turned out to be a pre-release copy of the 2005 "Crossing the Event Horizon" seminar that was completely riveting and incredibly exciting physics. Was this the main science that I had steered totally clear of in high school? Of course there was also chemistry; in fact, to be truthful, all the sciences scared me. What a difference 40 years makes.

To my total delight and fascination, Nassim Haramein has discovered the Golden Grail of Science that had eluded Einstein and the physics community ever since. Nassim's version of the Unified Field Theory, which is the same physics for the infinitely large (Newtonian) as well as the infinitely small (Quantum), also unifies the sciences. What a concept! He has found that the key is through geometry – sacred geometry - and also includes information from ancient sacred texts.

Once self-educated and driven by 9 year old epiphanies of how the universe works, Nassim has persisted until collaboration finally arrived to open the doors to the Sacred Halls of the International Physics community.

This arrived in the form of a well-respected and retired female physicist by the name of Dr. Elizabeth Rauscher from Berkley. Together they wowed and rocked the world of those Sacred Halls. So much so, that in September 2009, Haramein was awarded the "Paper of the Year" peer-voted by the international physics community at the annual conference in

Belgium. What an astonishing achievement! The paper simply states that our universe is a black/white hole of creation and that each of our human cells is a black/white hole of co-creation. A black hole absorbs energy; a white hole explodes energy to create. These are two aspects of the same phenomenon, once thought separate. Haramein has mathematically proven that our human bodies are "the Event Horizon" between the infinitely large and the infinitely small. This means that science literally demonstrates how we are co-creating our reality with universal consciousness at the centre of our beings! It also explains and makes sense of "going within" for all the answers. Whenever I asked for a psychic reading the inevitable reply was that the answers were within me. Thanks a lot I would say, but what about my friend to whom you just gave a whole hour tape of information? More to the point, how do I access that gold mine that was supposed to be inside me? This was my frustration and became my quest.

I was so excited by Nassim's DVDs and live presentations that I travelled to learn more from him. I was subsequently privileged to be part of Haramein's first Certified Delegate program of his Unified Field Theory in 2009 at a most auspicious time: Halloween. I was in awe, especially as for one particular day he taught us the physics of Inner Resonance and shared his version of a transformative meditation, similar in concepts to my own.

Nassim Haramein was invited to present his work to the International Physics community in Belgium in August 2011. More details of his work can be found and supported at www.theresonanceproject.org.

Quantum Bleep Talk

"What the Bleep Do We Know?" was the "Little Movie that Could" and did rock the world. There are so many layers in this movie that every time I watch it I notice something new that I already knew! The main nuggets to come out of this movie for most people are that quantum physics is the science of possibility activated by our intention and emotions through our perception from past experience. The scene of the wedding reception with the cartoon features is hilarious in demonstrating this and graphically drives it home in our understanding. The other part that I feel had a huge impact in the consciousness of so many was the scene with Dr. Joe Dispenza where he talks about how we can intentionally create our day. A whole subculture has arisen from that scene by the fireplace. He teaches us that "the neurons that fire together wire together". This means that when we have experienced a beautiful piece of music, eating our favourite ice cream or with someone we like, then that music will be a potential switch in the future for craving ice cream or thoughts of that person; or perhaps when you see that person you will think of that song or decide to get an ice cream. Of course it works for all the not so pleasant and traumatic memories as well. Chemical memory in the brain works by associative triggers, which is why it becomes so important to clear the information in our mindfields of old pain as there are multiple unconscious environmental triggers to activate our past traumas.

For example, there was a man who crashed his motorbike and broke his knee. Down the block there was a tulip tree in full bloom. Do you think he consciously noticed this when flying through the air? Probably not, but his subconscious would have recorded all the details of the scene. We know this from subjects of hypnosis who when regressed give remarkable detail of experiences. This man's knee healed up pretty well, but he was going through the breakup of a relationship at the time and was out of work. Many years later his knee was fine and he was walking down a street on holidays in the beautiful springtime when he stopped to look at a tulip tree in full bloom. When he walked on, his knee gave out and he could hardly move. The pain was excruciating! With great confusion, he went to the doctor to whom he reported that he had not stumbled or indeed fallen or tripped. Upon examination the doctor said there was nothing physically wrong with his knee. It must be all in his head. It turned out that the doctor was right when he made this pronouncement. The information in his mindfield had triggered a memory through the associative trigger of the subconsciously recorded vision of the tulip tree all those years earlier when he broke his knee. Additionally, whenever he had relationship problems or was struggling financially, he would likewise get jabs of pain in his knee but never could trace the connection as it had never been consciously made.

That is another reason why IRT is so important: It clears out all the potential environmental triggers from the informational field that has been associated or connected in every way, shape or form with a particular issue, effortlessly and unconsciously, without having to bring it to awareness or re-experience it in any manner.

Playing the Field with Lynn McTaggart

"The Field: In Search of the Secret Force of the Universe" is one of those resource books that are so full of important information that give foundation to our quantum reality. It is required reading for my advanced students. Lynn has done a masterful job of not only interviewing many of the leading edge quantum scientists, but also weaving the piece of each person's story of discovery to make sense of the bigger picture of our greater potential. This book makes me think of those novels with a cast of characters that we see featured in special chapters which then get put together in a whole exciting story. McTaggart has done this for laypersons of quantum science. One scientist in her book, William Braud, conjectured that spontaneous remissions or instant healings could be the result of the person's future self, traveling back in time to redo history, resulting in an immediate impact on the body. This was fascinating to me as I had been doing this with clients for years as an experiment which worked for most people. Lynn's gifted reporting has switched on a lot of light bulbs to illuminate our journey as we play in her "Field". Her subsequent books, "The Intention Experiment" and "The Bond" expand on these concepts with experiential co-creative applications of this science.

The Heart of the Matter:
The Resonance of Heart Math

Did you know that we have more neurons in the heart than we do in our gut or brain? What I have learned is that the foetus starts as one big brain and then, as it grows appendages and opens up, the head houses the brain and the gut is the other end with the heart in the centre. The Heart Math Institute teaches us that the heart has its own neurological system connected into a specific part of the prefrontal cortex of the brain. What I understand is that when a thought or information from the environment reaches us, it hits the heart first, then travels up the spine into the back of the brain, the cerebellum, which then acts as a clearing house, directing the information to the appropriate part of the brain for the chemical pathways to connect to the cells a la Dr. Lipton's teaching.

The heart has an energy field shaped like a double torus (think figure eight in the round) that emits a powerful resonance that echoes the energy field of the earth and likewise the universe itself. If we are made in the likeness of God, then this is a perfect example of the fractal nature of the universe. There is a mathematical formula based on what is termed the Fibonacci Ratio which gives consistent proportion to all of life. For example each segment of your fingers is a third of the total length of your finger; your arm is one third of your body's total length and so on. The Parthenon in Greece was constructed according to these principles, resulting in one of the most beautifully pleasing buildings of all time. Everything in nature adheres to this basic formula from the lowliest plant up, resulting in the web of life. When my children were in preschool the teacher informed us that if we

37

measured our children when they were 3 years old and tripled that number, then that would predict their adult height. I had a hard time believing my youngest chubby, short daughter would grow into such a tall, lithe and graceful woman, towering over her sister and me! For more information from the Heart Math people see the Resources section at the end of the book.

When we breathe into our heart centres the body relaxes and our energy becomes measurably coherent, resonating the energy from the heart field outward in waves that calms all in range. Howard Martin of Heart Math demonstrated this with some of his technology in Vancouver. He had a stressed volunteer come to the stage and then simply asked her to breathe with awareness into her heart. The computer screen showed a remarkable shift from sharp, spikey lines into 'smoother' energy lines on the graph. Likewise when we are upset or scattered, those incoherent energies radiate from us, resonating with and attracting similar discordant people and situations. Our outward world reflects what is happening within from the principles of resonance.

In physics I have learned that the more coherent, or aligned, harmonized energy entrains lower energies upward to match the peaceful calm frequencies, unless there is too big a difference which then polarizes like oil and water. This is seen in relationships where one partner is growing spiritually but the other not. Unless the other decides to change, to match or at least accept and harmonize, separation becomes inevitable.

When we blame someone or something else for our reactions or situations, we do not understand that it is our own old 'stuff' that is being activated by the other, outside influence. Our old 'stuff' resonates outwardly and magnetically attracts similar experiences until we free ourselves up by clearing that unwanted past within our own being. We are co-creating with everything within us and around us in the bigger world using the principle of resonance.

GOD is Within Us, proves Gregg Braden

Gregg Braden's book "The God Code" is a spectacular read as he leads us through the discoveries that the four elements which make up the DNA correlate to the name of God in Hebrew and Arabic texts. Following is an excerpt from Braden's introduction:

"A remarkable discovery linking the biblical alphabets of Hebrew and Arabic to modern chemistry reveals that a lost code – a translatable alphabet – and a clue to the mystery of our origins has lived within us all along. Applying this discovery to the language of life, the familiar elements of hydrogen, nitrogen, oxygen, and carbon that form our DNA may now be replaced with key letters of the ancient languages. In doing so, the code of all life is transformed in the words of a timeless message. Translated, the message reveals that the precise letters of God's ancient name are encoded as the genetic information in every cell, of every life. The message reads: 'God/Eternal within the body'. The meaning: Humankind is one family, united through a common heritage, and the result of an intentional act of creation!"

This is one of many fantastic discoveries that are revealing our Oneness.

Of Water and Blood, the discoveries of Dr. David Schweitzer

It was 1996 and I just happened to be there once again when Dr. David Schweitzer came to do his first Vancouver presentation. It is my understanding that he had met a Vancouver based Live Blood Cell Analyst at a medical conference in San Diego who invited him to Canada. David was introduced to us as an MD who had practiced in Britain for 20 years as a blood specialist. Also special is that he is the grandson of Dr. Albert Schweitzer. He showed us several slides of the results of a negative and a positive thought form in a cell. We saw that a negative impact in the cell had all the molecules huddling together densely in an irregular, dark mass that did not allow the light to penetrate. This made sense both as a metaphor for fear and also as a real life understanding: Medical scans look for dense tissue to indicate disease in the body. When we contract, function decreases. To the contrary, a positive thought was shown to have a balanced, even distribution of molecules with a lot of light throughout. Dr. Schweitzer explained that as blood is mostly water, and our bodies have 70% water, then we are influenced directly by thoughts and emotions. He continued to develop his research on different meditational and emotional states to evolve ways to interact and influence the body for good health.

Crystals of Water: The Magic within Us by Dr. Emoto

On the other side of the globe, Dr.Masuro Emoto had also been doing similar research in Japan, but from a different perspective. I also just happened to be a member of Noetic Sciences when our Vancouver group sponsored Dr. Emoto to do his first presentation in our city. I will never forget either the slides or the humour of the delivery. What an amazing and entertaining evening! Dr. Emoto explained his process of freezing water to about -30C and then when it warmed up to about -2, it briefly formed crystals which he then photographed with special equipment. His process was to imprint distilled water with images, sound, thoughts and words. The same water was shown before and after being influenced, and the results were stunning. The pictures of polluted water from a single sample were transformed by simply changing the label with the words Love and Gratitude, which subsequently formed a most magnificent crystal! As the man in the subway station in the movie "What the Bleep" commented at a display of Emoto`s water crystal pictures of words, "Imagine what your thoughts are doing to your body!" I love the next scene where the lead character draws hearts all over her body then gets into a bathtub of water to positively influence and shift the frequency of her cells.

Doesn't this understanding make you think about all those slogans on the T-shirts that we wear and the tattoos people embody? I once was "tickled" by a T-shirt with the slogan: "Unless you are living on the edge, you are taking up too much room". I wore it everywhere. Guess what happened to my life? You are right! I went into survival mode, having barely enough.

Following the terrible earthquake and tsunami in South East Asia in 2006, I remember when the next stage of catastrophe was set to happen with water borne diseases, including cholera, being expected. Dr. Emoto sent an email to his global network asking for prayers of love and gratitude for those trauma riddled waters. A couple of nights after that email I happened to be watching the news when they announced that the secondary wave of destruction bringing cholera was not happening as feared. Astounding! Dr. Emoto's work is completely fascinating with many more examples of the power of our consciousness, especially collectively, to transform ourselves and our environments.

Back to Dr. Emoto's presentation: When we got to the section of slides entitled "Showing Pictures to Water" one particular slide was the most impactful of the evening for me. A bottle of distilled water was placed on a picture of an elephant. The resulting crystal was very blunt and hexagonal in shape which was interesting in itself, however from the top into the centre was the shape of a trunk; the defining feature of an elephant! How magical!

This phenomenon was similar to the image of a crab that appeared in sand resonating with the Crab Nebulae's "music of the spheres". I once read about someone who had been able to record the sound of the Crab Nebulae star system. When he played the "music" through a metal plate with sand on top, the sand organized itself into a picture of a crab - remarkable echoes of Dr. Emoto's work.

From that I was inspired to envision that if some people like Paul Armitage, a Vancouver based musician, could channel someone's soul sound, then perhaps that same musical information could be played through speakers installed in a sound bed with ear phones on the person, for binary left-right brain integration. That experience could potentially realign their energy field by resonating the body into harmony with the expression of their higher self. All that was dissonant within the person and their field could potentially be released. I felt that this would result in good health not just physically, but emotionally, mentally and spiritually.

I then heard of a tribe in Africa where the women take an expectant mother into the desert away from the village and channel the baby's soul song. When the child is birthed, there is a 'welcoming committee' that sings the baby its own song as it emerges. In later years if the child misbehaves or commits a crime, the whole community gathers in a circle with the person in the centre and they all sing his soul song to resonate and harmonize the person back to a healthy expression of balance. This certainly puts our current crime and punishment paradigm into some question.

Back to the Future with Deepak Chopra's Timeless Mind-Bridge to Ageless Body

Just the title of Deepak Chopra's early book, "Ageless Body, Timeless Mind" indicates our potential. It is our imagination, the bridging power of the mind and spirit that runs the body. This concept when taken to its logical conclusion leads to an idea of immortality. Truly, if the mind and consciousness have command over the body, there is no need to age. What if aging and death were programs of belief rising from the unresolved built up experience of stress and negative thoughts and feelings impacting and contracting the body's ability to keep regenerating with full healthy capacity?

Deepak Chopra conducted an experiment that put volunteers into a movie set immersion environment where one week was relived from the 1950's. The people wore the styles, ate the food, read the newspapers, watched the TV shows, and listened to the music sitting on furniture from that period. He tested the participants' bio markers before and after with significant differences in anti-aging.

Indeed, some Inner Resonance clients have dropped ten years from their appearance and one was even seven pounds lighter in a one hour release session. Talk about a weight loss program! Negativity and depression physically weighs us down and ages us. For a dramatic impact of stress we need only look at U.S. presidents even early in their term, but especially after four years.

I believe that aging is the default program of the physical without the freedom of the spirit to be fully engaged in creating and recreating its joyful expression of life in healthy balance.

Receiving those Chopra tapes right at the beginning of my search for understanding of what I had stumbled upon and put together continues to be an inspiration for the possibilities of Inner Resonance to contribute to that long sought after "Fountain of Youth".

I am convinced it is within; somewhere in that still dark place at the centre of our universe in each cell, driven and informed by our consciousness. Shift our consciousness: Extend our lives.

Mind Power

Have you heard about the experiments using mind power to build a "six pack"? A Couch Potato's dreams come true! There were two groups being studied. One group did the exercises as usual; the other group only imagined doing the same routines. The results were surprising: There was only a minor measurable difference in the benefits of muscle tone and strength - Remarkable! Of course athletes have known this for a long time as they train in their minds for that competitive edge. That is how the Russians "cleaned up" all the Olympic Gold Medals in 1972. Now this is common practice. Remember, the body does not know the difference between real and imagined and responds as if. Have you ever watched a dog dreaming? "Google" Dog Dreaming YouTube for an excellent and humorous example.

In 1996 I was in practice in White Rock, BC with a Naturopathic Auricular Acupuncturist. A golfer came to us for treatment who was entered to win a million dollars in a Hole-in-One contest. The Naturopath did ear acupuncture and I helped his bodymind remember the other hole-in-one experiences he had achieved, and also to go into the future event and see and feel the success, both of which he then anchored into the present time within himself. This resulting chemical signature was then programmed into a brain switch to activate the automatic hole in one contest success. Inner Resonance helped him to also clear any anxiety and doubt that would interfere with his win, and to create a clear pathway to his goal. He focussed with clear intention, keeping that chemistry activated on a daily basis. The evening of October 14 was a good one, except the golf tournament booked prior to the Hole-in-One event had run overtime. This meant a single shot in the dark for all the contestants who were after that million dollar prize. All the big sponsors were there and it was impossible to rebook on short notice so off they all went to take their turn. Sadly, because of the conditions, no one found the hole in the darkness. However, our client won the contest as the one closest to the pin. No million dollars, but a win nonetheless. I considered that a success story for IRT. What I learned from that event was to also consciously create all the conditions surrounding the event for optimal success and to actually see the money in his bank account; not just general success but all factors desired.

Body Power

Our bodies are so incredibly intelligent, in fact, miraculous. Scientists are now growing organs from the person's own adult stem cells in labs. First of all an organic scaffolding is constructed, often made with pig's gut which is very compatible with human bodies (no comments please), in the shape of the particular organ and then dipped in a mixture of the person's blood. The stem cells seem to be informed by their environment (what was it that Dr. Lipton taught us?) and proceed to make a whole working organ. I saw another TV documentary program on Knowledge Network recently which showed the technique of taking an organ from another body and removing all the DNA material to be merely a ghost of its former self. Then once again that 'skeleton' was dipped in a solution of the recipient's stem cell material which then produced a fully complete working organ that could be transplanted into the person's own body with no fear of rejection. I know I keep using that word amazing! It really is beyond amazing!

Bodymind Power put to work in new ways.

What science tells us is that we all have adult stem cells that produce the ongoing cellular regeneration process of the body. What if, instead of the automatic program, the mind could interact with the system to direct the stem cells to specific areas of the body and "tricked" into speeding up? Remember the power of prayer? Gregg Braden reminds us that the highest form of the power of prayer is to see the end result with all the feelings of relief and joyful gratitude that our imagined goal is already accomplished.

I just happened to be there in 2000 at the first Prophets Conference in Canada, held in Victoria, BC when Braden showed a film of the 2 minute and 32 seconds that it took for a kidney tumour to be dissolved before our very eyes on an ultrasound monitor. During that time 3 men chanted and envisioned a healthy kidney, while the patient focussed on gratitude. This took place in a hospital in Beijing, China.

> *"This way the entire information was transmitted without any of the side effects or disharmonies encountered when cutting out and re-introducing single genes from the DNA. This represents an unbelievable, world-transforming revolution and sensation! All this by simply applying vibration and language instead of the archaic cutting-out procedure!"*

Excerpt from an article "Russian Discoveries of DNA" from the book "Vernetzte Intelligenz" von Grazyna Fosar und Franz Bludorf, ISBN 3930243237, summarized and commented by Baerbel.

Stroke victims who have lost the ability to move one side of their body are often taught to set up a mirror on the affected side and move the healthy arm and hand in usual ways. The "mirror neurons", as they have been named, believe the illusion that the damaged arm can move and respond to reprogram the brain, restoring full function to the damaged side. When I was delivering a mini pilot research program for the North Shore Stroke Recovery Groups in Vancouver, BC I learned that the initial paralysis from the brain to the body is temporary from the physical trauma. In time, the body can actually move again, but the brain is programmed to believe it cannot. This reminds me of the elephant baby who is restrained by a simple rope, appropriate to the youngster's size and strength. The adult animal could easily break that constraint but does not even try as the brain is programmed to accept the limitation. The body believes what the mind perceives.

Chapter 5: The Inner Workings of Inner Resonance: The Seven Step Protocol

So how do we put all this together in a way that we can use to effortlessly transform our lives with purposeful intention? Fasten your seatbelts! Prepare to be underwhelmed.

This is a disclaimer before reading further. Just by reading this you may find you can throw away your crutches if you are confined by a recent or historical injury. You may break out in a peaceful state that takes you unawares. Someone might call you and offer you the job of your dreams. Really! And all so organically and effortlessly that you might not even notice; believe it or not.

I like to give the example of two older ladies who are going out for a walk. Mabel is having a hard time with her arthritis flaring up. As Martha waits patiently for her friend to shuffle along, she notices a paper on the ground. It happens to be a page of IRT protocol someone from my class has dropped on their way home from my workshop. Martha picks it up and Mabel says, "What's that you're reading?" Martha reads it out loud, trying to make sense of it herself and they both decide it is a bunch of gobble-de-gook and throw it in the corner trash can. However, all of a sudden, Mabel straightens up a bit more and is walking more comfortably, the pain gone. It may be that Mabel continues to be free of that pain as her subconscious tapped into the opportunity to heal. This is how non-invasive and profound Inner Resonance Technologies is. The capacity is within and knows how to respond automatically. The protocol carries its own frequency; a built in morphic field of its own intention.

"I won a session with Maureen in a benefit auction and, after much procrastination, enjoyed a most inspiring session with her. I was dealing with personal issues relating to friends and family, and came away with an uncharged perspective which resulted in easy resolution of those issues and more. I have experience with hypnosis, Educational Kinesiology, Touch for Health, the Forum and other modalities. All of these have been of use and have helped with my personal growth, but none are as easy or universally applicable as Inner Resonance. In sessions, I have accelerated the healing of skiing injuries dramatically, improved my golf game, and best of all, silenced the little negative voice in my head that examined everything I said or did to make sure it was inoffensive. I now, mostly, live comfortably in the present and speak directly from the heart, and when circumstances create tension that might pull me away, I use the touch-breath technique and feel myself settle down. What a blessing. I have encouraged many sceptical friends to try this work and have enjoyed their successes. The work is so subtle, that sometimes people forget their issues so completely that they don't think anything happened. What wonderful bodies we have that can respond so completely at an energy level, and how fortunate we are to have Inner Resonance to help us tap into our personal magical powers! For me there are no limits to the possibilities, and I enjoy the potential for greater growth every day!"

Alice Jennings, awjennings@shaw.ca

I had one client who came to see me and insisted that the only way she ever processed with any technique was to know and understand the issue before letting go. I asked her if she would be willing to let go of the pain around the situation first

56

before she had the information and understanding in order to access the information with less resistance. Then I would be happy to do regression work with her to find out what had happened to create this problem. She agreed but re-iterated that she would definitely need to know and understand. That was the only way she processed. We finished the clearing work and I asked her if she was ready to find out what it had been about, and she looked at me, astonished, as though I had just grown two heads and said, "Why would I want to do THAT?"

This demonstrates just how effortless Inner Resonance is ….people do forget because the healing is so rapid and so complete that it seems to redo history automatically in people's minds. Because they have not reinforced the awareness with hard sustained work and effort, the conscious mind is less likely to notice. Like not having the flu, we forget the pain as we are designed for health and joy, our normal state.

What follows is a manual for practitioners that anyone can apply and benefit from. Of course most people prefer a collective, supportive group environment where experiential practice with a trained facilitator is helpful. If you can benefit from this book as it is presented here, that is wonderful.

As the chapter title suggests, there are seven steps in the Inner Resonance protocol that form the concepts that can be languaged in your own way. To start with, words are given as templates with which you can practice.

Before the steps are shared, I would like to include some frequently asked questions that may give an additional context from which to understand Inner Resonance Technologies:

Is IRT like Reiki, coaching, counseling, Jin Shin Do, any other modality or service?

No. IRT is a catalyst for all other modalities to make them even more efficient.

What is a catalyst and how does IRT do this?

A catalyst is an element that is added to something, activating change and then is removed, itself remaining unchanged.

By shifting the underlying root core causes and everything that has become associated or connected with the issue wanting help, IRT activates the individual's own system to rebalance and harmonize itself physically, emotionally, mentally and spiritually.

What is IRT?

Basically, IRT has 7 steps in which you set the inner conditions and agreements that allow your system to re-activate the built in programs that have been interrupted by stress or trauma of some kind, switching on the body-mind's innate ability to rebalance and harmonize itself by clearing out those interference patterns.

What is an interference pattern?

An interference pattern is information stored by the system to protect you from being hurt. When the dangers are over, these protections become blocks to your system being fully functional, using up considerable energy on storing these outdated memories. They become patterns of automatic, reactive behaviours, inappropriately expressed.

What conditions does IRT help?

Physical:
From simple injuries to serious, chronic and terminal illnesses, IRT empowers you to activate the self-healing regenerative programs of the body through the power of the mind and spirit, which have command over the physical, human world.

E.g. Arthritis, asthma, cancer, surgeries, accidents, addictions, Irritable Bowel Syndrome etc…

Mental/Emotional:
Because every thought or emotion has a chemical signature in the system, IRT helps to create a chemistry of wholeness, allowing pathways to get switched back on. By clearing the pain or "charge" from old memories in the body-mind systems, clarity, insights and information are available with more objectivity, allowing healthier, more productive choices. This results in achieving more of your potential.

E.g. Post Traumatic Syndrome Disorder, trauma, sexual abuse, stress overload, addictions etc.

Spiritual:

When confusion and old pain are released, new found clarity leads to freedom to know and express more of whom you truly are, feeling connected and whole, sometimes for the first time. This brings meaning and inner peace to all parts of your life.

E.g. Feeling confused, lost directionless, unknown purpose, lonely, disconnected.

How many sessions do people need?

Normally, 1-4 sessions (of an hour or so) are helpful for the main issues that need help. However, you decide how many sessions and how often they are appropriate. Because this is such an empowering model, from the first session you have the tools for continuing your own process on a daily basis.

Is the benefit permanent or do the issues come back over time?

For most people, the issues are resolved permanently, but only your system knows what it can handle at any given time, so everyone has a different response. You are however, equipped with tools for self-healing to keep "peeling off the layers" as needed on a daily basis.

Who attends your workshops?

Other professionals:
Coaches, addiction specialists, counsellors, hypnotherapists, etc. who want both self-care tools and a catalyst for moving their most challenged clients through those resistant, stuck spots rapidly, with ease, grace and self-direction.

Massage therapists, Jin Shin Do practitioners, physiotherapists, chiropractors, naturopaths, yoga and fitness instructors, etc. to help their clients release chronic patterns in the body-mind, allowing faster response and more successful treatments.

Individuals wanting to transform their lives and possibly help their family and friends.

Individuals looking to develop a career in the self-help/healing arts.

And now to the main event: The seven step Inner Resonance protocol to fully unleash your unexpressed evolutionary codes and activate your magical self, effortlessly...

Step One:
Breathe and Remember Who You Are

Remember you are already breathing: and breathe, easy... whatever that is for you right now, knowing that is the breath of your consciousness, connected into universal consciousness, the source of all possibilities.

This is who you truly are, a limitless, timeless spiritual being, co-commanding your reality with greater consciousness.

What is Universal Consciousness?

There has been talk about the smallest indivisible piece of matter, called the adamantine particle, sometimes even referred to as the God Particle, which is found everywhere: in and through all things including the air; even in deep space once thought to hold nothingness. The bigger truth is that the tiniest possible particle is still infinitely divisible. It will be interesting to see how many larger Large Hadron Accelerators will be built before this truth is known and accepted.

This cosmic building material is intelligent and responds to thought:

> *"It is the stuff of which all things are made."*
> See Wallace Wattles' book "The Science of Getting Rich

Information travels INSTANTLY in this cosmic field. This action is sometimes referred to as "non-locality" as it operates outside of time and space as we normally experience the linear physical world. Einstein called this "spooky action at a distance".

For example, at a talk by Gregg Braden, author of "Walking Between the Worlds", "Fractal Time", "The Isaiah Code" and "The God Code", I learned of an experiment that was undertaken.

There were volunteers who were trained to emotionally respond to both horrific and 'warm fuzzy' pictures. Scientists had equipment present that could observe the action of a DNA molecule when a negative or a positive emotion was experienced. A negative response was observed to create a tightening of the double helix spiral, much like a spring, whereas there was a relaxing, elongating of the 'spring' of DNA when positive emotions were experienced. Ever heard the expressions 'up tight' or 'hang loose'? Interesting how our language reflects what is literally happening in our bodies.

I understand that one of these 'subjects' volunteered a piece of skin (DNA) from his hand that was then put into a Faraday Cage, which is designed to insulate anything inside from any electro-magnetic energy waves outside this box.

The box was then moved progressively down the road, away from the volunteer's body, who at each stop, emotionally responded negatively and positively.

Each time, both 'host' DNA and the disembodied DNA responded simultaneously in the exact same manner, no matter how far away they moved the DNA. They finally stopped after 50 miles, as there continued to be zero time response difference. This same experiment has been repeated over many thousands of miles.

Remember what we said, information travels INSTANTLY in this 'non-local' field!

It is the same thing when you 'know' who is on the other end of your ringing phone.

There are 'masters of consciousness' like Sai Baba, reported to 'create' real, material things, instantly, out of thin air: e.g., think 'apple' and make one appear in his hand right away!

What one man can do, all people can be trained for.

All of us are evolving our consciousness to be able to do the same things:

Take for example, fire-eaters or fire walkers. At one time very few could do this 'magic' of walking on hot coals. Now, it is becoming an everyday miracle, with people showing up in droves for an afternoon or evening all over the world, having a few short hours of training and doing the same thing without getting burned!

How is this possible? There is a physical law regarding fire and flesh is there not?

There is another universal law that says: Consciousness rules over the physical body.

The body does not know the difference between real and imagined.

Ask anyone who has just woken up from a terrifying nightmare, heart beating, panic stricken in a sweat, hyperventilating. Was the dream real or was it 'mind over matter'?

This leads to the conclusion that different and sometimes contradictory things can be true at the same time: We are moving from an 'either/or' universe to one of 'and, and, and...' as our understandings expand to include multiple layers of 'truth'. In other words, many apparently opposite things can be true at the same time.

"The Matrix" and "Total Recall" movies demonstrate that what we 'plug into' mentally and emotionally rules our body's responses. Our mind rules our bodies, real or perceived.

So coming back to Universal Consciousness, what are some of the qualities of this quantum field of 'God Particles' that some people might name 'Spirit'?

- An ocean of infinite potential, an informational field of possibility: the Universal Wide Web; the origin of creativity and inspiration.
- No limitations of time or space: all time, past, present and future are here in this moment, right HERE, right NOW.
- No limitations of the physical world. Consciousness rules over the physical. The body does not know the difference between real and imagined. It responds 'as if', a pure responder to consciousness: Mind over matter; Spirit over mind. Spirit trumps all.

In conclusion I would offer the hypothesis that as breathing units of consciousness, we are spiritual beings having a physical experience, not the other way around as we have been taught.

This being true, we then have access to this limitlessness of which we are a part.

This then becomes our birthright: This is who we TRULY are.

Rita was an older woman who came to me for treatment of her asthma. She was on steroid puffers and had always had trouble breathing. In her session she had an automatic insight that when she was in utero, the cord was wrapped around her neck, suffocating her. Also her mother was asthmatic and so that little baby had to compete for life and oxygen. After that was released, she came to the awareness that "there is always enough air to breathe" and never needed her puffers again. That was in 1997 and she is still breathing freely.

Step Two:
Plug in to your Power Source

From this place of awareness of your Higher Self, invite whatever you feel you are connected with in that greater reality that supports you spiritually. This can be done in your own way in your own time within yourself.

That's just great to know who we are and what we carry within us, but how do we access this limitlessness? Believe it or not, it is as simple as acknowledging, inviting and allowing all the support that is always there for us in our personal spiritual beliefs.

Has anyone heard of prayer? Scientists are conducting lots of experiments on the power of prayer these days, Dr. Larry Dossey being one of those researchers.

Remember that 'thinking' stuff that permeates all things, even the air we breathe?

Remembering who you TRULY are, as a spiritual being having a physical, human experience, not the other way around, INVITE SUPPORT from this higher source of intelligence, whatever names you put to it! Whatever that life-force energy is that makes our hair and fingernails grow. You are alive. Source IS: your birthright.

**Keep it simple: "Higher Self and Spirit, YES!
(you have permission to help and support)"**

This is like plugging in the power cord on your computer.

Keep the request general if you like as intention, as Step 4 deals with the specifics in greater detail.

Step Three:
Switch on the bio computer,
which is voice activated.

Feel where your body touches the world around you. Remember you have one, as sometimes we dissociate from our bodies as they are too painful. Activate all the programs that have been disconnected or have lain dormant by giving it a verbal command. "Body, Switch On."

The body has innate intelligence. It knows how to keep you breathing, digesting your food and circulating your blood, for example, without you having to tell it what to do or even to be aware of it. It happens automatically and unconsciously most of the time.

We are breathing in molecules of recycled atmosphere, each particle of which carries the memory of Creation. Simply put, the body is a communication device, a pure responder to consciousness: Mind over matter.

Olds cells are dying and 300 million new ones are being created daily without effort of the conscious mind. Each cell reproduces itself from the blueprint found in the DNA molecules inside the nucleus, once thought to be the brain of the cell.

According to what I have heard from Dr. Deepak Chopra, our body reproduces itself every year, with parts like a layer of skin forming every 5 days, a new liver every 6 weeks and a new skeletal system approximately every 3 months etc., etc.

We are like an incredible super computer; fully loaded with all these amazing programs we cannot even begin to dream about they are so complex! The body is this amazing communication device, connected into the Universal Wide Web (UWW) or super-consciousness. Have you heard of nano-technology? Nano just means tiny, tiny, tiny. One of the most advanced computers that I read about in Scientific American in 2003 is a nano bio-computer, which is the size of a drop of water and runs off a single molecule of DNA, such is the capacity of DNA to carry information. This computer needs no external source of power.

"The human DNA is a biological Internet and superior in many aspects to the artificial one. The latest Russian scientific research directly or indirectly explains phenomena such as clairvoyance, intuition, spontaneous and remote acts of healing, self-healing, affirmation techniques, unusual light/ auras around people (namely spiritual masters), the mind's influence on weather patterns and much more. In addition, there is evidence for a whole new type of medicine in which DNA can be influenced and reprogrammed by words and frequencies WITHOUT cutting out and replacing single genes. Esoteric and spiritual teachers have known for ages that our body is programmable by language, words and thought. This has now been scientifically proven and explained. Of course the frequency has to be correct. The individual person must work on the inner processes and maturity in order to establish a conscious communication with the DNA."

From the book "Vernetzte Intelligenz" von Grazyna Fosar und Franz Bludorf, ISBN 3930243237, summarized and commented by Baerbel.

This computer is self-powered: Wow! JUST LIKE YOU! Now think carefully about the next statement:

Our body has more than 5O TRILLION CELLS! A bigger WOW!!! Over fifty trillion times the capacity of our most sophisticated computing system! If that is not food for thought, I don't know what is. We are walking miracles! Well, anything we can build, we can do better ourselves!

The body is a communications device and has access to:
- The memory of everything from all times and places
- The programs and intelligence, connected to the UWW
  (The Field)
- The unlimited capacity to respond.

So how do we activate this amazing communication device, otherwise known as the human body? Have you heard of voice-activated computers?

Turn on your bio-computer in this simple way: SWITCH ON, BODY!

Remember you mostly run on the default level of automatic programs. This command is to wake up and activate all the programs and capacity than normally lie dormant or have been switched off.

Step Four:
Intention: Give a Command to the System

If anything were possible, what would you choose?

Remember ask and you shall receive?

Intention is vital in putting this power to work for you.

You can plug in and turn on your computer but nothing much happens until you make a request to the system from the keyboard. This is equivalent to the conscious 5%.

You can (and usually DO) delete old files on your computer without having to bring them up onto the screen to read through them first.

Much like a computer, you can be specifically general or generally specific.

For example: I choose to:

Delete all files and programs with the word "Pain" in it: physical, emotional, mental and spiritual. We hit "ENTER" and the "processor" does the work for us.

Or: Clear out this shoulder pain or clear out this emotional trauma.

Or: Clear out all beliefs and issues that no longer serve the highest good in this moment.

Choose what you want.

Whatever your issues are that you are aware of, be sure to also take the opportunity to include all issues that no longer serve any useful positive purpose, known and unknown. Remember, everything is here and available now in the timelessness of higher consciousness.

Address:
- All possible root core causes;
- All of everything that may be associated or connected with this issue (e.g. shoulder pain) on all aspects of my being: physical, emotional, mental and spiritual;
- All levels of memory: this life, ancestral DNA, soul and planetary memory.
- All aspects of yourself on all levels of reality in the greater cosmic wholeness

We are quite used to asking this of a computer's memory. However, that could be considered overwhelming for some of us, as we haven't been used to asking THAT big for ourselves, or even knowing it was possible. We have been functioning on what I call the 3D default, factory settings of the physical body and human reality, forgetting our Higher Selves: Remember, as Consciousness is timeless and rules over and commands the physical world, this can be instant!

I have found that making certain agreements with the system creates the safety needed, especially for the body, to allow what is possible to actually take place.

These following agreements also address certain collective limiting beliefs, and without invalidating those old beliefs, they simply invite openness to other possibilities. Newtonian physics was not invalidated by Quantum mechanics, but expanded upon.

Step Five: Licensing Agreements: Creating Safety

THE SEVEN AGREEMENTS

We make these agreements with our higher selves:

Would you:

1. Allow your own system and your higher self that knows best for you to select only what is safest and most appropriate for your highest good at this time? *This puts YOU in control. No one is going to do anything to you.*

2. Allow the whole process to be done throughout with gentleness and ease?
We are programmed for struggle from our past experience but we are designed for flow. "No pain no gain" is simply untrue. We also learn from observation and through joy.

3. Allow effortless grace?
This addresses the beliefs of "You have to work hard for anything worth having and you need to earn your way and deserve it". Effortless grace to be and express our full selves is our birthright.

4. Allow the parts that are appropriately ready, to demonstrate INSTANT, PERMANENT healing in order to show you the possibilities?
This bypasses the limiting beliefs of "no panaceas" and "beware the quick fix".

5. Respect and honour the parts that need time to process, while at the same time allowing everything to speed up faster than the normal, 3D physical expectation?
    Moves you into a deeper level of trust and acceptance of what IS, decreasing resistance.

6. Ask the part of you that is willing to be open to experiencing something different, never known possible before, to be in charge?
    This puts on hold the conflict, the inner argument between the known and the unknown.

7. Ask the part of you that knows how to do this for you, together with Spirit, to be in charge.
    This allows you to really let go, not having to know anything or do anything consciously.

That is all the hard work finished. Now we get to play!

Step Six: Would the Appropriate Modality Please Stand Up?

PROCESS

So what happens when you press "ENTER" on your computer? The processor goes to work for you as requested, automatically, while you wait for whatever time it needs to complete the task.

A screensaver, usually of your choice, comes onto the desktop for you to enjoy.

Now this is where your imagination comes in!

Imagination is the bridge that not only connects us to the Informational Quantum Field of Possibilities, much vaster than the Universal Wide Web, but also amazingly, creates the chemical shift in the brain to signal behavioural outcome in the body. See Dr. Bruce Lipton's description of this process in his book "Biology of Belief".

So the process can be as simple as imagining being somewhere BEAUTIFUL, PEACEFUL, JOYFUL, SACRED or all of the above.

THIS IS YOUR OWN 3D SCREENSAVER, A VIRTUAL VACATION.

Your ONLY JOB is to show up completely PRESENT in this place for as "long" as you want (timeless zone) with all the sensory input you can enjoy (without working hard). The objective of this is to take your mind anywhere, preferably a calm peaceful place, which occupies and distracts your conscious mind in order to allow your unconscious spiritual mind to do all the work.

If you need to help to find that peaceful or beautiful place try these tips:

- What are the details you SEE?
- What sounds do you HEAR?
- Do you SMELL anything exquisite?
- Are you TASTING anything delicious?

Occupy your mind with a good feeling place – this could also be a feel good movie, the Discovery Channel, imagining something creative that you enjoy, like beading, knitting, or going for a walk, or even actually engaging in any of these activities.

HOW DOES IT FEEL TO BE IN THIS PLACE?

This frees up your system to go to work for you outside of your awareness, without the interference of the conscious mind, which in its delusional, limited 5% thinks it can control everything.

Your "processor" is at work for you in the unconscious (95%), together with the limitlessness of universal super-consciousness where all things are possible:

RIGHT NOW, in THIS MOMENT.

Your system brings you back automatically, when the processing is complete for now.

CHECK IN ON YOUR ISSUE:

Is it gone? Can it be that easy and fast? YES!

A few people have even healed broken bones this quickly, believe it or not! I was more astonished than anyone, witnessing this phenomenon.

We truly are miraculous beings!!!

Everyone is different, so if the "3D Screensaver" doesn't DO IT for you, plug in another modality.

THE PROCESS CAN BE ANY MODALITY OR ANY THING, like going on a nature walk!

How can you imagine this issue cleared? Choose your process. Play with this.

Mind Body Magic and the Imagination Bridge to Everywhere

Here are some additional techniques for processing. You can use anything your imagination comes up with or any modality you know and like that works for you.

Mind Body Magic is the former expression of Inner Resonance which contains tools and processes that I have discovered and used. The best however is whatever you know or your own imagination suggests.

When you come back into the present moment after the initial process, and on checking in you find that the issue is reduced but not totally clear, then other techniques and modalities can be applied until resolution is reached or you feel complete for that time. Everyone is different.

Remember, these techniques are being used in the deeper and wider context of the Inner Resonance protocol which allows them a faster, more comprehensive and permanent effectiveness.

Visualization/Imagination

First of all, ask yourself how you would like to process next. For example you might ask if you feel the issue in your body. Where is it; what shape colour size texture etc. What needs to happen? Get creative here and allow the imagination full range to play.

Often body stress is perceived as knots, so just imagine any kind of knots and then untie them in your mind's eye. The body responds magically.

Imagining a waterfall washing through and cleansing your whole person is a popular process, as is floating or swimming in water.

Some people, especially artists love working with colour. They imagine the issue or part of the body that wants healing to be a certain colour, and then change the colour to a happy favourite one. When they check into the issue after this process, they are often surprised that it is completely gone. The brain takes the symbol of colour and translates that into the chemistry the body needs to shift.

Not everyone enjoys or is able to do this exercise easily. Remember that hard work is not the idea.

We have made agreement for easy and gentle, with effortless grace. You know what works best for you.

What is important to remember for all of these processes is that they are in the context of the Inner Resonance agreements so a reminder of your agreement for instant and permanent is important.

Pattern Interrupt

Patting is a good release as it interrupts the information stored and stuck in the body. We pat babies when they cry or pat each other on the shoulder to reassure that all will work out. This seems to be two energy fields bumping into each other, breaking up the stuck informational patterns, releasing what has been pent up. Just patting will work. If you are facilitating someone else, ask the person to let you know when to stop. Also ask for direction on the level of pressure used. This is good to use on many parts of the body. It does not really matter where as the memory is holographic; in other words each part has memory of the whole. Once a man was releasing anger and he asked me to pat his big toe. Strange, I thought at first. After the release, he told me that the last time he was really angry he kicked a big rock and hurt his toe, so the memory was anchored and associated there.

The thymus gland, just between the heart and throat is a good overall place to pat as that is where the immune system is regulated. This is especially effective for sadness and tears. If you wonder if you have the right place, it is the spot that sounds hollow when you thump while you are making a noise. This is a good one to teach children as they love the Tarzan version. This strengthens the immune system as well. I remember Gorbachev, the last president of the Soviet Union pounding on his chest while making a speech. If you are facilitating someone else, always ask permission before touching someone's body.

Pattern Interrupt with Sound

Another use of patting is to add sound, suddenly, which becomes a major pattern interrupt. The principle of sound for cutting through and breaking up informational patterns is very old and also used in current medicine. Doctors use ultrasound to break up kidney stones without invasive surgery. Inner Resonance has helped a few people to dissolve kidney stones with the power of their bodymind in just one session. A client in the early '90s had a stomach tumour the size of a grapefruit. She was also a very large person, who needed to lose weight before surgery was possible. IRT helped her melt the fat away and gave her time to "dissolve" her tumour to the size of a golf ball by the time surgery took place.

There are opera singers who, in hitting those ultra-high notes, have been known to explode crystal goblets. I knew a man once who had a very large crystal ball shatter when he held a concert in his house.

Then there are the old fashioned teachers that whack their yardsticks on a desk to get the class attention when out of control. The sound interrupts the patterns of chaos and brings everyone to attention with more focussed alignment…a natural shock treatment.

Martial Arts also use sound to help break up dense physical material together with the chop of a hand or foot. Using a sudden loud sound, such as popping of a balloon or clapping of hands or shouting a loud Martial Arts-like "kee-eye" chases the issue right out of the tissue of the body. People who claim to see energy fields have witnessed this and reported actually seeing the energy release.

One elder client in Arizona in the fall of 1999 had severe arthritis throughout her whole body, but concentrated in her hands and knees, such that she would be hospitalized periodically to give temporary pain relief as nothing else helped. We did a single 15 minute session using a pattern interrupt with sound on her knees following the IRT protocol and she was so startled with this natural shock treatment that she laughed for a long time, and then said, "You chased it out!" All pain and discomfort was completely gone from all of her body immediately. She remained pain free for the 3 years that I did follow up with her.

Another man who was in a group that I was giving a demonstration to was, unbeknownst to me, waiting for bypass heart surgery. He was first really angry about being startled by a balloon popping and shouted that I could have killed him. I responded with some depth of relief that it was a good thing that it did not! He never did need his surgery. By the same token I learned to warn people. It still has the same impact even if you pop the balloon yourself. Just remember to blow up the balloon to the maximum and hold the tied end down. Frustrated and angry children as well as adults, or those with ADHD, love this. I had to clear my fear of loud sounds before I could do this. It is effective.

Sound

Sound, real or imagined is another way to clear and rebalance the system using the Inner Resonance protocol. The only important thing to remember here is that any music used must be pleasing to the person healing themselves. Mozart has been studied scientifically and verified to create harmony and brain coherence. However if a woman's abusive ex-husband was a concert pianist, this most likely will not have the effect intended, but rather trigger more angst, anchoring it deeper!

There was a shopping area where undesirables hung out, intimidating the high end shoppers. One merchant had the bright idea of playing loud classical music outside, which had the desired effect of moving the challenging youth away. Their energies resonated with heavy metal discordant sounds which were dissonant to the more harmonic, coherent frequencies, and therefore really uncomfortable to the disruptive negative attitudes. The result was an oil and water effect, allowing business to flow once again.

Jane is a musician and highly sound-sensitive. Sometimes when she calls me for a session when "life happens", just hearing my voice answer the phone is her trigger to let go. The issue just dissolves as her brain associates the clearing process to the frequency of the sound of my voice. Recently her father died and as often happens in these circumstances, some childhood issues were triggered. She left a message for me when I was not home. Either hearing my voice on the machine, or just imagining talking with me triggered her own brain's chemistry to activate the Inner Resonance program she already had installed within herself, so that she sent me an email saying it was completely cleared. I have another person that calls me when I am not home to hear my recorded voice message as she has told me that she associates the sound with her own healing activation and feels better.

Movement

Sometimes the person needs to move in certain ways, so it may be that they go to a yoga class or for a real walk in nature, a run, or even dance. One client of mine had been going to the same yoga class for a long time. When a challenge came up in the body, they had an Inner Resonance session which did not appear to have any direct results. However, a week later in yoga class the body completely released.

This happens sometimes. Inner Resonance may clear the matrix of the person`s energy field but that individual may need a different time and process than is available in that moment to have completion of their issue. Everyone is different. At the most basic level, Inner Resonance clears the underlying causal levels to allow whatever intervention or process used to be accepted by the system, whenever it is ready, in the most efficient manner, permanently.

For a more complete list of secondary processes, I recommend that you read the book "Instant Healing" by Serge Kahili King.

I was told that the ancient Hawaiian Huna tradition, which I had never studied, had a lot of similarities to IRT. I discovered that over the years I had accumulated an almost identical list of processes to go along with Inner Resonance. There are many, many more techniques being developed all the time of course but that is what I love about this work: infinite variety. It is possible to have the same outcomes with any process, as the IRT protocol serves as a catalyst for all other modalities in existence, and those yet to be developed, to go deeper and wider with instant results, no matter how you are processing. The imagination is the limit, which is a limitless bridge between the mind and the body.

> *"Imagination is more important than knowledge.*
> *For knowledge is limited to all we now know and understand,*
> *while imagination embraces the entire world,*
> *and all there ever will be to know and understand."*
> Albert Einstein

I realized that IRT is like a prefix that clears and neutralizes the Field, or the Matrix of a person's charged experience from all times and places, including the ancestral and soul memory, on all levels of reality, simultaneously. Remember that consciousness includes all time and all aspects of reality in the Oneness that is here and available NOW.

The most important feature of this step is to keep checking in with yourself or the person you are facilitating whose imagination and experience has all the best answers for them. Working with others, you are there to support and co-create the process through their lead, facilitated by you. It is a dance that can be a lot of fun.

Inner Resonance is a catalyst that boosts ALL modalities into the quantum instant!

When you are feeling better, then you are running the program of healing:

THE CHEMISTRY OF WHOLENESS balance and harmony IS ACTIVATED throughout your mind and body, in every cell and fibre: Notice how this feels. Most people experience this as relaxation. Some people tingle.

Every state of being has a chemical signature present in every cell, and those cells are always talking to each other!

…..and they remember! Everything!!

"Esoteric and spiritual teachers have known for ages that our body is programmable by language, words and thought. This has now been scientifically proven and explained. Of course the frequency has to be correct. And this is why not everybody is equally successful or can do it with always the same strength. The individual person must work on the inner processes and maturity in order to establish a conscious communication with the DNA."

Excerpt from an article "Russian Discoveries of DNA" from the book "Vernetzte Intelligenz" von Grazyna Fosar und Franz Bludorf, ISBN 3930243237, summarized and commented by Baerbel.

Inner Resonance is more successful in this way as it asks for the specific frequency the body needs for the particular intention, and is inclusive of all frequencies in all dimensional realities. Healing gets "downloaded" directly and appropriately from the Field.

Step Seven: Reactivation Switch/ Speed Dial/Touch Breath/Short Cut

Because the body is a holographic system with universal living memory in each cell, (explained by the scientists Gary Schwartz and Linda G Russek in their book, "Living Energy Universe") you can program a One-Touch reactivation spot anywhere on your body.

This is like having a building wired for electricity and installing a light switch; loading a program on your computer and having an icon on your desktop for instant activation; or having a phone number programmed into a one-touch speed dial button on your phone. There is no need to remember the individual components but just have the programmed access point to activate the connection.

PROGRAMMING A SPEED DIAL

While still feeling great, choose a spot to touch on your body and at the same time be aware of all your good feelings. THIS IS THE CHEMISTRY OF WHOLENESS that you are asking all levels of consciousness to associate with that spot. Breathe in and out with awareness of both the touch and the feeling in your body.

Remember, chemical memory in the brain is released through associative triggers.

**The neurons that fire together wire together!
(What the Bleep)**

Whenever you touch that spot, and take a breath consciously with intent or unconsciously, the CHEMISTRY of

WHOLENESS WILL AUTOMATICALLY ACTIVATE, to heal and clear everything no longer serving a higher positive purpose for you in THAT moment of 'NOW', whether it is another 'layer' of the original issue or something different that is now ready to be processed. Remember, this does not need to be consciously known. Take a deeper breath and as you exhale, release your touch.

Remember, we are always a work in progress, never complete, but always moving into a progressively 'higher' state of consciousness. This is the journey.

I recommend that people use their 'SPEED DIAL' at least twice a day:

- AT NIGHT, just before sleeping: This activates an unconscious process to make the regeneration process and your dreamtime healthier and more efficient.
- IN THE MORNING, just as you waken. This sets up THE CHEMISTRY OF WHOLENESS to work for you automatically as you walk through your day, maintaining your system, much as an anti-virus and de-frag computer program runs in the background.

Of course, anytime you feel yourself 'triggered' or reactive, just touch that spot and exhale to have the issue neutralized, along with all of the root core causes, as well as everything associated and connected to all aspects of who you are, on all levels of memory, AUTOMATICALLY.

In other words, at a single touch and breath, you reactivate the combined chemical signature of all the steps and agreements in the original process. The more you use this, the deeper the conditioned response. The brain is a self-regulating pharmacy, responding to the bodymind programs.

Another use of the SPEED DIAL is to add to its strength by touching it every time you are doing something uplifting, whether it is a sunset, food, nutritional supplements, hugs, bodywork, healing of any kind, meditation or even medication. Sometimes people need to take medication, so this helps to filter the side effects, balancing the body around the medical drugs. This builds on the positive strength.

Anything good you do for yourself can be a process.

Sound too good to be true? Mother always said, *"The proof is in the pudding."*

Try it!

"The work is fantastic!"
Adrienne, North Vancouver

IRT Templates: A few suggested ways to language these concepts.

A Conversation to facilitate IRT

1. **Breathe easy.** Know that breath is your connection to Spirit/Higher Self/Life Force/ Universal Guiding Principle/ Source of All Knowingness and Love. Remember what you know about Spirit – it is connection to all possibilities and potentials beyond time and space, with command over all aspects of reality; freedom from time (past, present, and future are all available NOW).

2. Ask for help from 'Spirit' or whatever you feel connected to in the greater reality (may include spiritual helpers– guides, angels) in your own way, within yourself, taking whatever time your need. Let me know when you are ready to proceed.

3. Ask for help from your Body, that part of you that holds all memory, all intelligence, and the ability to respond to higher consciousness and limitless 'Spirit'. You can simply say– "Help Body" – out loud or silently to yourself. Let me know when you are ready to move on to the next step.

4. Intention – If anything were possible– what would you want, specifically or generally? Take time to reflect and

let me know when you have something in mind. You may say your intention out loud or silently to yourself. Would it be OK:

    a. To open the door completely wide to clear any and all issues that no longer serve your highest good?

    b. To clear all static and interference, hindrances or obstacles, to expressing all that you can be?

    c. To include all possible root/core causes; everything that maybe associated or connected to this issue - physically, emotionally, mentally and spiritually?

    d. To include all levels of reality, all personalities, all dimensions, all frequencies of the greater cosmic wholeness?

5. Agreements – Will you allow this process to be:

    a. Done with gentle ease and effortless grace?

    b. Safe and appropriate at all times?

    c. Instant and permanent for what is ready at this time?

    d. And for what is not ready, allow yourself to surrender to accepting that everything has its own time and let that be perfect in the big picture that you don't know.)

    e. Ask the part of you that is willing to be ready and open to a new possibility to be in charge?

6. Process - I invite you now to take your conscious self to a place that is safe, relaxing and pleasurable where you can be in total comfort and ease. You may imagine yourself in a beautiful scene in nature or in a happy, pleasurable experience in a peaceful colour, light or soundscape. What do you see hear smell taste feel? (Facilitator: consider integrating here any secondary modality at this point – bodywork, Reiki, homeopathy, traditional counselling, nutritional support, essential oils, etc., etc.)

While you are in your safe, peaceful place know that your subconscious is automatically processing and acting on your intentions, within your agreements, together with limitless Spirit, beyond time and space.

Take whatever time you need.

When you are ready to check in, open your eyes.

How are you feeling? If not complete, then the secondary processes can be used. You can ask, do you want to go back to that safe place to allow more to process or would you like something different…don't like imagining? How about Pattern Interrupt? How does your body feel? Where are you feeling it? What does it look or feel like? What do you want to do with that?

What kind of pain? (E.g. Hot or sharp or dull or throbbing) work with the metaphor….ask what they want to do to shift that. Remember the imagination is the bridge the brain uses to change the chemistry in the body.

How are you feeling? Keep on asking after every process until complete…

7. Speed Dial:

What do you feel and sense in your body?

Are you complete for your process, for your intention?

Notice again how your body is feeling: This is the chemistry of wholeness.

To anchor this feeling, choose a spot on your body to touch and notice this touch, along with the feeling in your body and your breath. When you have all three streaming in your awareness, take a breath with your touch and breathe out through your mouth, letting go of your touch as you exhale. Do this 3 more times for a total of 4 to program this touch.

You are creating a switch in your brain to recall and reactivate this chemical signature of wholeness for anything else you need to release or want to create at any future moment.

Practice this touch-breath twice daily – last thing at night, on awakening in the morning are good times – and any other time you need a boost or get triggered.

Computer Analogy Process

1. Plug into your power source whatever Spirit is to you. Spirit, Please Support and Help! As you breathe, know you are part of a greater limitless Spiritual reality breathing your Self into a body, not the other way around.
   Higher Consciousness has 3 main attributes:
   a. Field of all possibilities and potential
   b. Timeless: Past, Present Future all available now
   c. Command over physical human reality

2. Voice- activate your bio-computer: Switch On, Body!
   Each cell in your body:
   a. Has access to the memory of everything;
   b. Is fully loaded with all the programs needed to rebalance and harmonize all systems;
   c. Has the capacity to respond to higher mind/power

3. Key in your intention:
   Ask for what you want to be free of or to create, in as much detail, or as generally as you choose. Widen this request to include all possible root core causes and everything associated or connected with these issues on all aspects of who you are, physically, emotionally, mentally and spiritually; include all levels of memory, all levels of reality

4. Licensing Agreements:

Will you allow:

  a. your own system to select only what is safest
  and most appropriate for you at this time

  b. the whole process to be done with greater ease
  and gentleness than thought possible

  c. whatever is ready, to be instantly and
  permanently processed

  d. whatever needs a different time or another
  process to be allowed to unfold in its own way

  e. the part of you that is open to this process to
  be in charge and work together with Spirit

5. 3D screensaver: Virtual Vacation/process:
Allow your imagination to take you on vacation. Your
only job is to show up completely present in the
moment of this place with as much sensory input as
desired. Your processor is at work at an unconscious
program level together with limitless spiritual help
beyond time and space and will bring you back when
completed by opening your eyes.

6. Save program to icon on desktop: Touch/ Breath
Touch a spot somewhere on your body, noticing how
the "Chemistry of Wholeness" feels, asking all levels of
consciousness to associate this spot with reactivating
this program when requested and clicked on. This will
automatically take care of whatever needs
reprogramming, rebalancing and harmonizing in
THAT moment. Breathe in and let go…do this 4 or 5
times.

Inner Resonance Technologies 12 STEP Process

1. Breathe easy, remembering this is the breath of life, the breath of consciousness that connects you to a Higher Power, greater than yourself: a Higher Power of timeless possibilities with command over the human, physical world. From this place of remembering your higher self, connected to a greater wholeness.

2. Ask for help from your Higher Power as you understand that to be.

3. Ask for help from your body, which has memory of all hurts and pains as well as the memory of innocence, together with the intelligence of how to bring you back to balance. Ask for help from your body, which knows how to surrender to your Higher Power.

4. Humbly ask for all the root core causes of all the pain and resulting fear from all your shortcomings and defects of character to be removed on all levels of memory, all aspects of who you are: Physically, emotionally, mentally and spiritually.

5. Ask to surrender only what is safe and appropriate for the highest good for all concerned at this time.

6. Ask for greater ease, gentleness and openness to the gift of grace as appropriate for this time and always.

7. Agree to allow what has no further positive, higher purpose to be completely released right NOW.

8. Ask for acceptance and surrender for what needs time to process on your journey to wholeness, allowing the grace of your Higher Power to walk beside you at all times, helping to keep you on the right path.

9. Ask the part of you that is choosing to be entirely ready to surrender to your Higher Power for your highest good to be in charge.

10. IMAGINE: A place of serenity/joy/freedom from pain and the craving need to medicate, a place where everything is possible.

11. Check in: How are you feeling? This is the "Chemistry of Wholeness".

12. Program in a Higher Power button/switch or Touch/Breath for the "Chemistry of Wholeness" to be re-activated daily and/or whenever needed for the work in progress.

Inner Resonance Technologies
Conceptual Skeleton for you to play with your own words.

7 Step Process Outline: Bare Bones

1. BREATHE

2. ENGAGE THE SPIRIT

3. ENGAGE THE BODY

4. INTENTION

5. AGREEMENTS

6. PROCESS

7. SPEED DIAL

Chapter 6:
How Inner Resonance Helps – From Addiction to Workplace Stress

Addiction

In my opinion and experience, when people are given an opportunity to clear the unconscious, underlying pain that causes addictions, then the need to self-medicate dissolves. When this happens and they are reconnected to themselves, their gifts automatically activate and meaningful purpose fills them up, allowing the person to become more whole and at peace.

Maggie's story

"My mom had a heart attack January 22, 1991 the day after my birthday. After she was stable, I went to my parents' house in Vancouver and drank too much. Even so, I got behind the wheel to drive home to Surrey. Exhausted and emotionally drained I started to nod out on the Alex Fraser Bridge doing 85 mph.

I believe it was angels that woke me up just before I hit the meridian: I careened all over the road, across three lanes of freeway. That moment is when I made the promise to the Universe, "If you get me across the bridge I will stop drinking." As I got closer to the end of the bridge I changed my mind as I realized that I had no right to risk the lives of others because of my addiction. So I amended my request:

"If you get me home, I'll stop drinking." Angels drove my car home as I was so inebriated and in shock.

The next morning, January 24th, I was assaulted by my partner for being away and not being there for his needs. I phoned my sponsor to cancel my agreement to go to my first AA meeting as I was so traumatized and needed to find a new place. He told me that everyone would be supportive…I could stay with him and his wife until I found my own place to live.

All day long I kept hearing a voice over and over again saying, "Someone will be there for you", to the point where I finally gave in. As soon as I agreed to go to the AA meeting, the voice stopped. Once you make the choice for your highest good the Universe supports you. I have been listening to divine guidance ever since. I listen and the magic happens….always.

I met Maureen at my first AA meeting that night of January 24th, 1991. She was there for her client's first birthday. I noticed that the man was at peace with himself compared to the other members of AA. I felt compelled to go and talk with her. She invited me to a workshop introducing her healing method in a small group. I was able to retrieve a traumatic memory of abuse by my mother at the age of six, in a pain free and liberating way. The weight of the world dropped off me. I had previously been in therapy for 2 years to help me understand why I was in such an abusive relationship. Maureen's training gave me a healing of recovery, understanding and remembering my life's journey. Having peace, love and forgiveness for who I am, I never needed to look back.

Maureen never did go to another AA meeting, so that one was meant to be, for sure. I have been blessed to share this healing work with many people on their journey from recovery to love.

I kept going to AA for another four months to support others who were into one day at a time. Maureen's work taught me to heal from the source of why I drank so I could understand, forgive and love myself.

I felt that the difference was that AA was one day at a time but your technique went to the source to heal the need for the lifelong emotional Band-Aid of alcohol and gave me freedom from the daily support needed to struggle and maintain that.

Thank you, Maureen, my Earth Angel and friend. Thank you for being you."

Love, Maggie. September, 2011.

ADHD

The father of a nine year old boy in Grade Three on Ritalin was kicked out of school into a specialized daycare as completely unmanageable everywhere in the school environment; constantly acting out in the classroom, in the hallways and even on the playground. To make things worse, his father was head of Special Education. After working once with the father and once with the son, the child was re-integrated back into the school after a long four day weekend. The boy went a full two weeks after our original session before there was a single incident that normally would have triggered a full blown uncontrollable reaction: Another boy bumped into him in the hallway. The child, on his own without adult intervention, apologized to the other boy and turned the situation into humour, making a joke of what happened. This astounded the staff who reported that he was like a totally different person. He was taken off Ritalin.

Another little boy in Grade One was having some challenges at home with an alcoholic mother who was taken away from him. He went to live with his father. This student was having regular conflict with the school bus driver and other children on the bus, and also could never stand in line and focus enough to order his lunch appropriately. After one session the boy was transformed, according to the adults in charge, including his father, who had also received a session before I worked with the child. The boy was able to self-manage after that without Ritalin.

Arthritis of the Spine: Ankylosing spondylitis

A female counsellor in her thirties came to Bowen Island for an educational retreat. I was called in to do some massage work for the group. I always ask permission to add in IRT, as the body responds so much faster, making my job a lot easier.

In this case the woman had ankyslosing spondylitis, a progressive, apparently incurable arthritis of the spine. In her first session she was pain free for a long time. She did have another 2 sessions when she felt her back starting to activate any symptoms. However, she remained free of her symptoms for the most part.

Asthma

"My name is Melanie Graham and I would like to talk about how the work that I have done with Maureen Edwardson has helped my asthma. As a child I never had any problems with asthma, although each winter I would get a very nasty bronchial cough. Then, in the winter of 1984, I caught a cold that basically was with me until very recently. I was working in a Head Start pre-school and had sick children on my lap much of the day, so couldn't get rid of the cold. I was also very emotionally stressed out, and running quite a bit, so I got overtired, I guess. It was an exceptionally cold winter, so I would breathe in cold air and this must have really damaged my lungs because I developed bronchitis, pneumonia and then the asthma from there. It took the Doctors quite a while to diagnose, because it was so sudden and no-one in my family had ever had it before, but it was definitely asthma. At one point I coughed so long and so hard that I cracked a rib, which was horrible.

I have always been a very physical person and having asthma really put a damper on my physical activities, at first. Once I got connected with my Dr. Paul Creelman, about 10 years ago, he put me on a medication plan that kept my breathing clear. For several years I took Prednisone regularly, from 5-

40mg, depending on how I was feeling. I even got pregnant with my first child while on Prednisone, and was very uncomfortable with this. Even though everything turned out alright, I vowed to myself that my next child would not be exposed to any steroid medications through me. So I slowly weaned myself from the Prednisone (from 1990 – 1991) and was free of it by the time I became pregnant with my next child in the winter of 1991. I was still using my "breathers" regularly…a Vanceril inhaler and a Vancanase AQ nose squirt. For all of these years (from probably 1987 – 1997) I took 3-4 puffs of each of these medications 4x every single day. If, for some reason, I did not use a breather for a couple of days then I was fine for 2 days. On the third day my breathing would begin to tighten up and I would be in trouble by the end of the third day. I also have a Proventil inhaler that I would use whenever needed.

After working with Maureen on Saturday, 8 November, my medication plan has changed dramatically. I keep waiting for my Doctor to call me and ask why I am no longer filling my prescriptions! I was a regular at the local pharmacy for many years. Directly after being with Maureen, I had 3 days of very severe asthma, tough to breathe at all, and I needed to use the Prednisone to sleep at night. Slowly, however, this tightness began to relax and my breathing was easier, clear in about 5 days. On Friday, 16 November I spoke to Maureen on the telephone and she supported me in my choice in stopping my breathers all together, which I had not done for 10 years, ever since the asthma in my body was diagnosed! Amazingly enough, my lungs were fine. One and two days passed, and then the telling third day. Well, that day passed by also and I was fine. My breathing was really fine without any medication at all! About a week after that, I had a glass of red wine at a party and really felt my chest tightening up, which scared me. I went back on the breathers for a couple of days and then off again for almost a month and a half. So the entire month of December I was not on any asthma medication at all. I teach school full time, and in the winter months I work for the US Forest Service outside (teaching people about Bald Eagles) so at this time I was on my 7 day a week work schedule, along with working out at the gym 3x a week, and raising two children alone. Even with this busy schedule and physical activity, exposure to the elements, I was really fine. At Christmas time I was exposed to an awful flu bug and caught it really bad. I was very sick with a horrid cough and the asthma returned. I had to get back on my medication very diligently and it took almost the whole month of January to get myself back under control.

On 29 January I went back off the asthma medication. The flu bug was finally gone, and I had killed the bacterial infection with antibiotics. This, I made it the whole month of February without any medication and now it is well into March. I worked again with Maureen recently, on 6 March, concentrating on my allergies and trying to heal those problems. It has been one week since then, and I am still able to walk outside without too much discomfort. Occasionally I will use a puff of the Proventil inhaler at night, but I am feeling pretty comfortable during a time of year that usually knocks me flat."

Allergies

"I came to see Maureen in the middle of 2010 spring allergy season as I was suffering greatly like I had done for many years. I had been recommended by a friend who had received relief with Maureen's work the previous year. With only one session of Inner Resonance, I have not had allergy symptoms since. This is late July of 2011 and I have been totally allergy free this year in a long wet spring and late cold summer which has produced an intense allergy season for many others."

Erin, Bowen Island, BC.

Anxiety

"Hi Maureen~ I just want to say THANK YOU for the work you have done with me. It is beyond belief how things are changing for me. Immediately after our first session, I found a new place to live and the landlord at my new place is thrilled I am renting and letting me move in early for my convenience. My son & granddaughter are going to try to come and help me move. I am better able to understand people objectively/no hurt or anger. This is most astounding as I was the complete opposite.

I am coping better with all my relationships and know when I need more clearing. One of the most wonderful things to happen today is that I feel so peaceful as I have carried extreme anxiety most of my life. My childhood trauma and the recent loss of my husband are no longer haunting me. I have a whole new level of freedom to be my joyful creative self and am doing more writing and beadwork again."
Naida, West Vancouver, BC

Broken Bones

Amy, a petite but feisty woman was afraid when her partner came home drunk one stormy Friday night. Their fight turned physical and the big bear of a man kneeled on her chest to confine her, not realizing in his inebriated state that his body weight was crushing her. The next day the hospital confirmed she had 3 broken ribs and probably more would be revealed in subsequent X-Rays once the swelling had gone down. I was called in Saturday afternoon. She was bruised and swollen and could hardly move or breathe without excruciating pain. After a brief 10 minute protocol, her pain and swelling had subsided. Remarkably, the bruising also changed to a more advanced colour. The doctor, puzzled, assumed there had been a mistake. The next day, on her own, she righted a pine log frame that had blown over in the storm, and continued to tan her buffalo hide. She also chopped wood later that Sunday.

I love the story of a good friend of mine, Jan Furst, an old Norwegian man. Two years ago at the age of 97, he was backed into by a truck and knocked over. To give you an idea of the man, he tells the story that it was he who bumped into a backing truck. He made his way home only to find out three days later that he had a double compound fracture of his back. I moved in to take care of him as normally he lived a vital and independent life. Within 6 weeks, he was fully recovered and even better than before the accident, as he took the opportunity to do his physiotherapy and massage along with Inner Resonance (what he jokingly called 'witchcraft') every two or three days. The doctor was 'flummoxed' as something like that would normally be the end of someone his age. Instead he improved his balance, strengthened his muscles and most important of all, rebuilt his confidence. What a guy!

Business

"In life, as in business, it is often difficult and challenging to connect the 'dots'. In this case the work we did with you and resulting road that our business has taken seems to be in this sphere. I believe in the philosophy of your work and the underlying impact on the direction and resulting path that I it helped to put our business on. Our business has taken an entirely new direction and I cannot help but believe your system did not impact this process in many ways. Our team is working together better than we could have hoped for and our business is tight and focused. We are all so pumped up about where we are and where we are going. I recall that you emphasized how your system would begin working once we completed our sessions with you and continue working in some underlying sphere that does not cause lightening response but with time would be significant and I have to say it is exactly what has happened. Our success, it seems, is only a short distance from where we are today and we are very happy that it is with good conscience and creativity that we have found our calling in the business world and your work was definitely a part of this. Thank you Maureen for helping us to get on the right path!

Kerri Groves

kerri@lookout-software.com

604 730 9801 (phone) EXT 3

Updated story......10 years later.

"Well Maureen, since the brief time we spent together nearly 10 years ago I have learned more about business than I ever wanted to. After some time, our software company began to collapse around us and I had to start another business to keep one programmer afloat as we struggled to get to another platform and reinvent ourselves once again. Everyone else in the company lost their job. Approximately 5 years ago we decided to go to a different platform, essentially starting over. Our massive financial investment in the original software development put me near financial ruin and I didn't know how we would hold on to anything – including our home. The day we were ready to launch our new product we scraped together $350 for a web site and immediately the leads started coming in. It was going to take 3 more years before I could stop the transitional business that had kept me from living on the streets but today we are growing again. The horrendous debts I incurred during those years are paid off and we are selling our new product to companies around the globe. The future looks very bright for us. Along this 8 year journey of transitioning the software business I faced enormous pressures that I am forever grateful are behind me. Somehow dogged determination kept me believing we could succeed but looking back I am amazed at it all. The lifestyle I currently enjoy is fabulous and something I could not have imagined as now I have downsized to work from home in a relaxed environment with clients all over the world who have become a community of friends. What a far cry from the old business paradigm into this new level of freedom."

Residual Inner Resonance has taken her through some tough times bringing her into a whole new ideal world. I can't help but wonder how it might have been even easier and faster if she had continued more than one session with Inner Resonance...although she would not have learned all that she did and understood just how powerfully resilient she is. There are gifts in all our challenges.

Carpal Tunnel Syndrome/ Chronic Pain

"For the past 2 years I have suffered with carpal tunnel that affected my hands, wrists, elbows and on up to my shoulders. To avoid the surgeon's knife, I have been getting acupuncture once to twice a week for one year plus I have had six months' worth of agonizing serious deep tissue massage that has been absolutely excruciating.

After my first treatment of IRT and massage with Maureen, my joints felt 95% better. After the second treatment, I can happily say my shoulders on down to my fingers have not felt this good for as long as I can remember.

I have also had a chronic pain in my lower back that seems to have always plagued me no matter how much stretching or chiropractic work I have done. Maureen took me back in time to discover that the pain was caused by a fatal knife wound from a past life. She "removed" the knife and the energy attached to the incident that has been stuck in my auric field and my cellular memory all this time. The spot where the knife came out has been transformed and is no longer in a big tight knot.

This healing has changed my life, physically and spiritually in ways I would never have imagined. The best thing, I know this healing keeps on working long after the session is over.

It is life changing and I would recommend it to anyone that is ready to let go of all the old 'junk' that

no longer serves a purpose and is causing pain, physically, emotionally and spiritually."
Colleen Gibson, Surrey, B.C. Canada.

Epilepsy

When I was in Russia in 1995 I had the opportunity to stay in the small village of Kurai in the Altai Mountains of Eastern Siberia, 100 kilometres from the Mongolian border. Eight of us Westerners were there for a week and just as we were waiting in the bus shelter for an imminent departure in fifteen minutes, our interpreter came rushing up with two old men. They were desperate for my help as they both experienced seizures a couple of times per month and wanted healing. I did not know if I would ever be able to help, however I took them through a brief protocol with Galena's translation and then boarded the bus, regretting that I would never know the outcome.

Surprisingly, our translator Galena travelled back there the next summer, at which time they raced over to her expecting that once again I was with her. They wanted to tell me that in the following year after our brief intervention, they had only had one seizure each. Incredibly, for the first time in her life, that next September Galena travelled outside Siberia for the first time - to North America and we met again when she reported their follow up story. Life is an amazing journey.

Fertility

Two women that I facilitated have been successful using Inner Resonance for conceiving and having babies after long-time efforts had been unfruitful. One woman ended up having twins, and the other had artificial insemination that was successful…so successful that she had a second baby in the same way!

Fibromyalgia

"In my early 30s I began to notice some worrying symptoms: vertigo, muscle pain, insomnia, memory lapses, confusion, feelings of dread, being overwhelmed. Over a 14 year period the symptoms increased dramatically yet no-one could help me. I was told I perhaps had arthritis, was too uptight, that it was "all in my head". By the time I met Maureen I was a very sick woman and had finally been diagnosed with Fibromyalgia, a chronic auto immune illness that does not have a cure and for which Western medicine cannot offer any real help. The day I was to meet with Maureen I left my home dizzy, nauseated, "fuzzy" minded and in such pain it hurt to have anyone touch me. I felt hopeless and helpless. Maureen welcomed me into her warm, inviting space and introduced me to Inner Resonance. With her calm voice I was led through a session that proved to be the beginning on the road to regaining my life: Gentle, non-invasive and best of all, immediate. I left her home a new woman ~ swinging my arms, moving my head, stepping out with confidence! The pain instantly went from an 8 out of 10 to 0 and has consistently stayed low since. The very next day I began a life-long practice of Qi Gong which furthered Maureen's miracle. Five years later I still reap the benefit of Inner Resonance. I have made changes in the way I live and am able to do so because Maureen helped me open a door. The combination of Inner Resonance and Qi Gong has enabled me to fully participate in life. Even when I'm having an "off" day I can use the tools taught to get back on track. I have a little "memory trigger" that I use whenever I feel Fibromyalgia rearing its ugly head. I am so thankful to Maureen for introducing me to this wonderful healing technique; she helped me find my life again!"

Kathy, Bowen Island, BC.

Grief

"In the last four months of 2002, I lost my beloved son and five more members of my family. I was devastated and it was only through my family, friends and strong spiritual beliefs that I was able to carry on. However, I had a hole in my heart like a crater which didn't seem to heal properly and on special occasions connected to my son, it was deep, searing pain of grief.

In 2006, on the fourth anniversary of my son's death, I was blessed to reconnect with Maureen who gave me an incredibly effective Inner Resonance treatment and I am happy to say I have never again felt that deep searing pain of loss. Through one session of IRT I healed my almost overwhelming grief once and for all and what an amazing feeling of relief. It was the most wonderful and astonishing treatment session I had ever experienced and I will never forget that life-affirming gift.

Yes, I still feel loss and sadness at times, however never again have I felt that incredible pain.

Thank you again Maureen, from the depths of my healed heart."

With much love and gratitude,

Maggie Gold, Vancouver, BC

Heart

Helge was a master chef forced to retire early. His heart was functioning on a mere 9.8% capacity and so he was put on the list for a heart transplant, not a common thing at that time. After one pattern interrupt session with sound, his heart improved 44% and he was taken off the heart transplant list. What happened that day is that he had an insight around an emotional broken heart because of a huge fight he had had with his father 35 years before. The very moment he was in the process of releasing that heart break his father started calling him, spontaneously after all that time, and they were re-united. A year later a second session brought another 10% improvement. He is written up in the Norwegian medical journals as a miracle. I certainly enjoyed the seven course seafood dinner he served up as a thank you!

Another woman in her 40's was tested for a possible heart transplant at St. Paul's hospital in Vancouver, Canada. She was tested all day Tuesday, after which I was called in by a friend to do a session with her that same evening. Wednesday they did another battery of tests and discharged her at 3 pm as her heart was 44% improved over the previous day. She then took a 6 hour bus trip home at 5:30 pm that same day and called me from work Thursday morning. I was astounded.

Hyperthyroidism

"In the summer of 2009 I was diagnosed with Hyperthyroidism. I was not interested in conventional treatment and decided to pursue a complementary/alternative healing course of action. I was scheduled to test for my Tae Kwon Do Black Belt in December of 2009, and so had extra motivation to get myself well for that event. In addition to changing my diet and pursuing a course of healing with my doctor of Traditional Chinese Medicine, I also worked with Maureen, as I believe her Inner Resonance Therapy technique is incredibly supportive and helpful no matter what other modalities one may be using. I also feel that my IRT treatments deepened the effectiveness of the other work that I was doing. IRT feels like the glue that kept everything else working together from a deep foundational place. From my work with her, I gained deeper peace and confidence in addition to clearing the underlying factors of my dis-ease.

After the first session I could complete my Marshall Arts routine for the first time in a couple of months easily and normally, whereas before I was not able to draw a full breath and my heart rate was through the ceiling so I had to pace myself. Amazingly, after that first session I could, literally overnight, fully engage in my training which was essential to my goal. This was huge!

We did a total of 4 sessions, with one more booster just before the test, more for extra confidence and focus as my strength and health was good.

In December of 2009 I successfully tested for my Tae Kwon Do Black Belt! I was also symptom-free of the Hyperthyroidism and continue to be so. This has been amazing and I am very grateful to be healthy, strong and happily in pursuit of my art and life."

Titania E.A. Michniewicz
www.titania.ca

Scoliosis

"As a publisher I believe in really understanding my author's work and so I have spent many hours with Maureen in private session around many old beliefs that I didn't think were movable. One of my major health challenges that I have had since childhood has been scoliosis of the spine. I had spent many hours understanding the meaning of 'being out of alignment' and the subsequent decision of my parents at the time to opt for my back to be broken in an operation that would 're-align' my spine. I was 'stuck' in the cycle of believing that because a steel rod had been inserted to support my straighter back, that I could not do traditional physiotherapy or exercises to strengthen my spine. I always considered the rod as preventing me from strengthening my own spine, and as a result I have suffered chronic pain since the age of 18. Maureen took me through an Inner Resonance session with a beautiful visualization exercise where I saw a different result from the operation resulting in a stronger, straighter and pain free back. Since this first session I have been using the touch breath technique every time I get back spasm and I now enjoy doing Yoga without fear of the rod preventing me from doing the movements and no longer let fear of other therapists 'touching' my back prevent me from receiving other treatments to release old tight muscles. Maureen has changed my life with inner resonance and I now accept my steel rod as just another energetic element I can embrace instead of rejecting and fighting!"

"Several months later I was with Maureen at the Edmonton Body Soul Spirit expo which was a very stressful situation for my back; concrete floors that I had to stand on for ten hour days with very little time to rest. I woke in the morning bent over with the pressure and stress and as I hobbled through the exhibition halls, Maureen was doing a quick process for me. She had pointed out that 'lack of support' could be more responsible for my back pain than my scoliosis or steel rod and that I was possibly triggered by previous expo's: with very unpleasant results 10 years previously when I lived in England. As I am muttering under my breath 'yeah right...' we approached the booth and one of the other authors smiled and greeted us warmly. I apologized for being late and leaving him alone at the booth to which he replied 'no problem, why don't you ladies go and have a good breakfast and I'll hold the fort'. My back physically straightened on hearing these words! It was a complete breakthrough for me! Yes, Maureen was right! It was not old beliefs around my operation - it was old beliefs around lack of support from other people! I was amazed to see the physical manifestation of the new support with my back straightening immediately - which really does prove, mind over body!"

Julie Salisbury, Influence Publishing

Weight

Many clients have had success letting go of extra weight using IRT. One man in particular comes to mind as ever since his late 20's he had tried every diet known to mankind and then some. He had been a telecommunications worker so he envisioned replacing the communications cable between his brain and his stomach, as he said his current one was not working correctly to send the messages to his body that he was full. I met him a week later at an event and just as I reached him to ask how it was going, another man came bounding up and said, "Joe, you look great! Have you lost weight?" The body had balanced itself and re-adjusted his metabolism to automatically start reducing.

Workplace conflict

"We have had the distinguished pleasure of working with Maureen on a personal as well as professional level. Introduced first by Carnegie Business Group, we worked as colleagues available to solve the challenges of Dale Carnegie's corporate clients by referral.

A few months back we expressed privately to Maureen our challenges with a client whom had recently undergone corporate management change at the highest level. Conflict was rife and affected our level of success. After much stick handling with the client and using every resolution technique known to our team of experts, we came to the conclusion that there was not much else to do except perhaps walk away from the contract. Not wishing to give up easily, we contracted Maureen whom I consider to be a "Professional Corporate Healer".

After being introduced as such to the principals at our client, they agreed to meet with her. After only 2 hours, and just the initial consult, all three partners seemed to change. Change within themselves as well as with others. Miraculously we were able to continue with the contract and resolve their issues. The client became so happy with our work that they even agreed to continue with a maintenance program with us for a full year.

We continually acknowledge Maureen for her source of commitment and healing abilities. Because of these and her extraordinary professionalism and sensitivity to all situations, we recommend Maureen highly and encourage everyone to inquire and use the power she shares."

Sincerely, Pauline O'Malley CEO, The Revenue Builder

Inner Resonance as a Way of Life

Everyone has their own journey. Inner Resonance is not just about instant and total healing, although that certainly does happen for many people. Our soul is having an experience and in that light there is truly no right or wrong way to 'get better'. At some level we are all choosing how and when and there is a bigger picture that none of us knows, mostly as we are co-creating it all together as we go. There is an intricate relationship of all things, and so Inner Resonance has the philosophy that everything is perfectly imperfect. We are choosing such a rich variety of experiences that come with many gifts.

What follows is a beautiful example of how Inner Resonance works together with everything in perfect ways for what the person is ready.

A Bumpy Beginning...

"When I first came in contact with Maureen Edwardson and Inner Resonance Technologies in January of 2011, I was at a point in my life where I seriously wondered if I was going to be physically able to even minimally fulfill the inherent life purposes I had felt so strongly the past 35 years, let alone take care of my basic needs the next few years to come, and I was only 54 years old!

In stating my true feelings here in spite of controversy or ethical concerns, I truly understood why Dr. Kervorkian was such an instrumental force for some, as I myself was wracked with seeming insurmountable pain from head-to-toe for so long with so little relief, that life was beginning to seem purposeless, and I occasionally (fruitlessly) longed for a 'new body' at times since it seemed my 'old body' was going nowhere fast.

The bulk of each day after every seemingly endless, purposeless, day was spent trying to manage the pain with minimal results despite maximum input from the best healing resources known for years on end, coupled by a sincere desire to let go of 'all which was not me at the core' and feel truly happy & alive again on all levels.

Life's passions and purposes were temporarily obscured in a haze of bio-chemical discrepancies, confusion, and a full loss of hope, with all joy just slowly slipping away as my body did the same.

Past History, Current Pain...

Providing a quick history on the reasons I was dealing with such severe and unresolved back & neck pain, over three decades ago, a drunk driver ran a red light at 100 mph and forever changed the state of my 19-yr. old body upon impact. Fortunately, I survived, and began a very long journey toward optimal healing. Along the way, I refused the offer of permanent disability benefits as I didn't want to apply such a label to my healing efforts, as I had every intention of healing the 'permanent' disc damage and resolve & release my ever-present companion, pain. My dear old dad, a scientist, professor, and thriving life-enthusiast, had forever impressed upon my mind & heart the phenomenal capabilities of the most magnificent technology on earth, the amazing human body! Feeling fully equipped for the task, I set about healing my body.

At the time the accident occurred, my parents were in the middle of a very sad divorce and struggling with their own issues, so my young adult self did her very best to put things back together and heal left-over injuries upon release from the hospital post-recovery.

Treasured Life-Learning...

Since that life-altering day in 1975, I have personally studied and applied myriad viable healing modalities, both individually applied and in the company of healing-oriented individuals of a scientifically-proven holistic variety, and always with the intent to heal at the core and empower the body-mind to fulfill the measure of its creation as a self-healing organism.

Each step in this beautiful journey offered ongoing relief and a semblance of progress toward greater well-being. However, even with full belief backed-up by awareness and action, nothing seemed to reverse or heal the post-accident spinal-instability with its companion, debilitating nerve-compression, and well-meaning medical doctors could only offer risky, unproven-surgeries and drugs.

Having been raised by a scientist-father who understood and exemplified the optimization of human potential, I chose not to believe medical doctors when they said things like "Plan on feeling miserable for the rest of your life." and "Due to the pelvic injuries, I wouldn't plan on having children as you probably cannot conceive and safely carry at this point".

I went on to bear a lovely family of sweet children, and any spinal pain was well worth the joy! Having safely carried and delivered each child, I was further convinced I could heal my back as well.

Present Day Dalliances...

Flash forward 35 years; and the holism I initially engaged in as a 20-something had blossomed into a greater measure of quantum understanding and application. That said, I had no idea how such lofty principles could actually offer the down-to-earth solutions (soulutions!) required for my hurting body, heart, and psyche.

Coming full-circle, prior to utilizing the principles of 'inner resonance', due to unmitigated, ever-worsening pain with rapid manifestations of body-decline, I found myself swallowed up in a perpetual abyss of fuzzy-thinking, confusion, and overwhelmedness, always on the verge of fresh tears.

As I prayed and meditated on this matter one day, my inner-knowing -- that part of myself which yields to the silent promptings and subtle whispers of all things divine -- was telling me, "This has been a great treasure hunt and given you lots of experience and empathy, and take heart! Next on the agenda, we will employ a simple system which ties it all together, brings it to the next level, and sets full-healing into motion!"

Armed with this internal nudge and assurance that this 'system' could be found with my fingertips at the computer, I felt gently guided to Dr. Bruce Lipton's "Resource Site", and found Maureen Edwardson and Inner-Resonance Technologies waiting for me there, and it's been a non-stop 'onward & upward' ever since!

The Sighhhh Response...

After my first phone session with Maureen, I noticed a few major differences.

It was as if nearly half the overall pain had lifted, instantly allowing me to sit for the first time in years without incurring a migraine or going into 'pain overwhelm'. I could not explain the pre/post-session difference at the time, but in retrospect, I think our session had a permanent 'de-amping' and overall relaxing effect on my entire organism, relieving muscle tension, nerve-compression, and thusly, preventing migraines and other compressive-issues. In general, I felt as I had somehow near-instantly reached higher-ground, and the view just keeps on improving!

I had a new sense of sustained energy and clarity -- the type of thing you usually feel after the perfect vacation -- which has stayed with me since then. It's like a permanent 'ooomph' that just keeps on 'ooomphing'!

This new sense of enhanced inner-acuity and naturally heightened well-being ushered in much-needed strength to act upon clarified intuition. This influx subsequently proffered a rapid flow of healing facilitators / facilitation, which further yielded perpetual progress and expedited results where once there was only stagnation and discouragement. The ball of tangled factors blocking the healing response was beginning to unravel, gratefully so!

Next, a brief rendering of such insights, progress, and results...

New Insights:

Much to my surprise, after years of entrusting my body's healing to holistic doctors (as the prospect of surgery and organ-destroying pain medicines held little appeal to me) I was being 'nudged' to see neuro-surgeons/orthopedic surgeons and this initially made me a little nervous!

I had watched my own mother's decline and demise following back-surgeries and addiction to pain medicine, and after checking in now & then with ortho-docs through the years to peruse the latest and greatest, I had pretty much written off anything "Allopathic America" had to offer.

It was now necessary to move through any 'fears' or apprehensions and follow attuned and heightened inner-guidance and play "Meet the Medical Docs!" and with a beautiful outcome!

Yielding to guided-action led me to amazingly 'open', in-tune, and love-centered neuro/ortho surgeons who surprised me.

One shared, "We now know that it is next to impossible to improve upon the healing mechanisms nature provided us with. As doctors/researchers, we are currently placing more of our research emphasis on ways to employ those mechanisms instead of disrupting them with the scalpel."

These same leading-edge neuro/ortho docs applauded my utilization of holistic principles and said such things had kept me happy, relatively healthy, mobile, and ALIVE! They encouraged me to keep it all up

My newfound strength and more finely-tuned clarity led me to doctors of a more quantum genre to continue to support me on the path kindled by achieving greater inner-resonance.

Interestingly enough, quite through 'happenstance' I crossed paths with an MD who practiced medicine in Asia for over 25 years, and came to America offering a magnificent skill-set which included the rich heritage of generational healing in the tradition of Chinese High Priests and Master Healers, including acupuncture, chi gung, advanced herbology, therapeutic massage, and all other ancient Chinese healing methods which facilitate and support (rather than usurp!) our body's healing mechanisms. It is my belief that the Chinese have been innately imbued with the knowledge of 'quantum healing' for centuries, and she confirmed this to me when I asked her the qualifying question, "Sooooo, doctor, can this spine be healed?" To which she replied, without missing a beat, "The spine will heal when the mind relaxes and allows the healing to occur."

As well, I 'found' an osteopath who, among many gifts, specializes in supporting activity of our innate and oft-times overlooked healing mechanisms.

As a result, I have reached an all new level of well-being I never thought possible, as for the first time in my life, I am allowing my body the healing time and unfettered energy that probably 'should have' been engaged in 35 years ago! In this new & improved horizontal position, there is but a mere shadow of the pain I use to endure. During my 'down-time', I am also more fully allowing any old feelings that may have been repressed during that or any other time period to more fully surface and release, an ongoing process initiated decades ago.

Surfacing awarenesses and 'letting go' of old healing-impediments leaves me lighter, more free, and with energies to spare, more fully aligned and enlivened than ever before! Hope and progress abound...

Very personal Insights:

Although I have always tried to schedule in relaxation and live a conscious, peace-filled existence, in reality, as the eventual single mother of five children post-divorce, my life was too busy for me to TRULY relax for years on end.

And wow ... an increased sense of surrender was when all new insights came rushing in! Now, it seems, I am being pleasantly 'forced' to relax my body full-time, and finally giving 'permission' for "me to take care of ME!" fully and unequivocally, without a fight! After enjoying caring for others first as a wife & mother for a decade, followed by 25-yrs. of single-parenting, then as a therapist for 13 years, it's now time to fully address ME, guilt-free!

As a motivational add-on, a rehab doctor told me, "If you don't address this NOW, you will find yourself very old ... very fast ... as in immobilized or dead." Great impetus which further encouraged me to allow my healing to be my one & only 'job' for a while and a joyful priority as I relax, pay attention, and take action! This very fulfilling 'job' comes with the excellent benefits of:

Feeling perpetually, with greater clarity and energy for healing and loving life, and wondering what type of progress new MRIs will yield down the road?

Current MRIs I felt nudged to get not only revealed a high extent of purportedly 'unhealable' spinal issues, but shed light on accident-related brain-health discrepancies with further action required and desired. With plans to follow inner-guidance as shared, I am engaging in 'quantum healing' for greater brain health as well. I'm so glad I paid attention to the nudges encouraging me to see these neuro-docs!

I feel as if erroneous beliefs & feelings which created internal static & blockages that circumvented my body's innate intuition & healing mechanisms were loosened, revealed, and released, allowing for all new healing progress.

With the pain-puzzle unraveling, life began to feel less like it was spinning out of control and more like the centered, joyful affair it was planned and intended to be!

I feel a stronger sense of Self and more fully understand my needs on every level, from the physical to the nuanced spiritual. I know on a core level that perpetual self-sacrifice, while a noble gesture to some, rarely does much to build health and long-term well-being! I have slowed my life and expectations to currently include only that which is of love, regeneration, and healing, and the 'right' people keep showing up to assist in this beautiful undertaking as I continue to create my future by knowing my present 'needs' and allowing resolution.

I more fully trust my inner-guidance or intuition as this past half year blossomed exponentially in all regards as I listened and applied these heightened, clear insights

Perhaps the greatest thing of all? I am at pure peace with my current state-of-being, knowing that no matter the outcome (which of course I feel will yield a more fully healed spine!), I know I will be able to manage my life and earn my keep.

Among other things, as if by magic, 'the right people' keep showing up on my door-step to help my second business get up-and-running after closing the doors of my first business due to body-decline three years ago.

As I follow what I feel, each day brings new gifts of all kinds to joy's threshold. More fully resonating with both my inner-self and all of life, I look forward to delivering my next life-affirming update thanks to the intuition and inertia set into motion with the application of this simple, powerful process known as Inner Resonance." Angela, California.

Most of the time, categorizing results with IRT is difficult as the benefits are many and global from each session. Even if there is one presenting symptom, many issues get addressed and resolved simultaneously. Here is another example of Inner Resonance as a way of life in this regard.

"Maureen first worked with me in July, 2011 helping me with a throat condition that had bothered me for nearly a year off and on and every day since February. Between February and July I had anywhere from five to ten or more episodes a day. It would start with a scratch, then a cough. Sometimes I would have dry heaving, then my nose would start to run, my eyes would water, all the while coughing. Each episode would last about fifteen minutes, then it would settle down and I felt fine again. There was no medical reason for this. It appeared to be allergies though no testing was ever done.

After the first session with Maureen the number of episodes I experience reduced to one a day and sometimes for a few days with none. I followed Maureen's instructions and did the breath/touch each morning and evening and sometimes in between for the next few weeks. After a while my throat problems were gone.

During that first session with Maureen I also worked on my high blood pressure. There were three more sessions with Maureen through the summer and when I visited my G.P. my blood pressure was normal and has remained so.

In September, 2011 I was in a car accident. The car was a write off and I suffered internal bruising and a broken sternum. After another session with Maureen my internal bruising eased off, and after two weeks I was hardly in any pain. I was told it would take weeks for this bruising to surface and heal. I was also told that my sternum would take at least six weeks to heal and maybe longer. However I have had no more pain or discomfort since the first week after the accident.

I was put on blood pressure medications two years ago this November and even then my blood pressure was never at the right level. Although sometimes it was lower than others, it is only since Maureen worked with me that it is really down. Even right after the accident when you would expect it to be over the top it was not too bad and returned to normal within a couple of hours. Paramedics were amazed, considering the adrenaline pumping through my body.

I continue to use breath/touch on a daily basis and find it helps me with not only the physical but also my mental outlook.

I am very grateful to Maureen for all the time spent with me and the lessons taught and will continue to work with her."

Lindsay

These are but a few examples. Inner Resonance is unlimited in its application and ability to help any condition or circumstance in your life.

Chapter 7: Your Journey Making the Intangible Tangible; A Medicine Wheel to Track the Trip

Healing and change happen whether we notice it or not. However, we know that what we focus on we create more of. You know how many paintings you get for your fridge when you appreciate and praise your child's art work. Our subconscious is like an inner child that loves to please you and create more of what works when we acknowledge the good: especially when we can focus on gratitude. That seems to be a major key in bringing more goodness our way.

When we track our progress and successes, we always have a place to reflect and remember how far we have come, and to give us hope in those times that seem to be an unending dip. We can see and be reminded that the patterns of our lives always spiral upwards when we are on a conscious journey.

Inner Resonance can be so subtle at the same time as having momentous impact. The effects are multitudinous and affect every area of our lives, no matter if the intention has been quite specific or general. The medicine wheel format is useful for us to reflect on how we feel, what we are thinking and doing and how we are responding to the bigger feedback loop of the Universe. We are then reassured by our own experience that the journey is a forward one with purpose in the larger context of our lives.

We are all different in how we express ourselves, so the following journal format invites you to use colour, draw pictures or symbols in all four areas of your life as you Track your Trip. Enjoy the journey of your joyful, effortless transformation! Use the simple template to create your own ongoing journal.

Highly recommended is that you have a journal for at least 4 weeks of awareness. Remember that the subconscious mind likes the number 4: The first time to check things out, the second and third time to be accepted by the logical and emotional parts of us, and the fourth for greater integration. I would encourage you to continue drawing your own pages after that in a continuous acknowledgement of the magic power you have within to change your reality. I suggest starting the first two pages with an assessment of where you are right now in order to fully appreciate your transformation.

I would be very grateful to receive feedback and news of your transformation and successes using the information in this book by email at **maureen@innerresonance.com**

"At its most fundamental level, the Medicine Wheel teaches us that in order to live a good life, we must show up and engage in it.

We must be mindful of how we treat each other, Mother Earth, as well as being responsible and accountable in all our commitments.

Mindfulness which means staying in the present and acting in non-judgemental ways creates an entrance to our souls, where our life's journey starts on a path of seeking the truth of our existence."

Shannon Thunderbird, Tsimshian First Nation
www.shannonthunderbird.com

Date:

Body

Mind

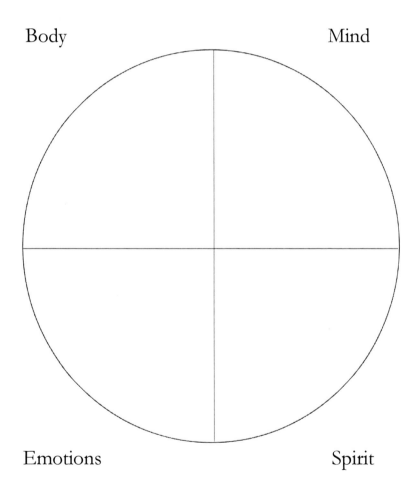

Emotions

Spirit

What have you noticed differently today?

What are you grateful for?

What inspirations have you had today?

Are you doing your Touch/Breath?
- Daily Practice?
- When you get challenged or triggered?

Date:

Body

Mind

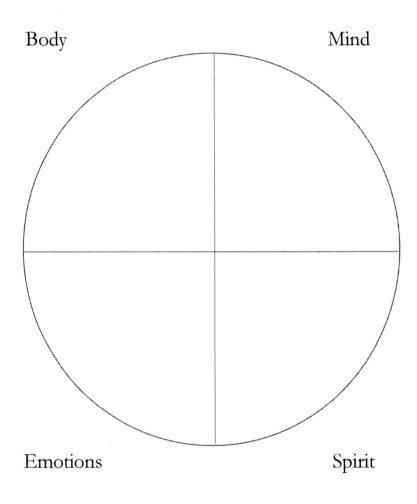

Emotions

Spirit

What have you noticed differently today?

What are you grateful for?

What inspirations have you had today?

Are you doing your Touch/Breath?
- Daily Practice?
- When you get challenged or triggered?

Date:

Body

Mind

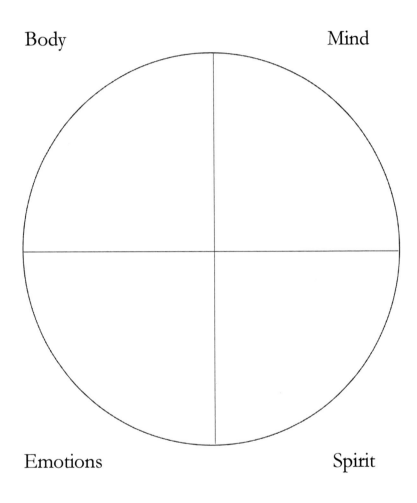

Emotions

Spirit

What have you noticed differently today?

What are you grateful for?

What inspirations have you had today?

Are you doing your Touch/Breath?
- Daily Practice?
- When you get challenged or triggered?

Date:

Body

Mind

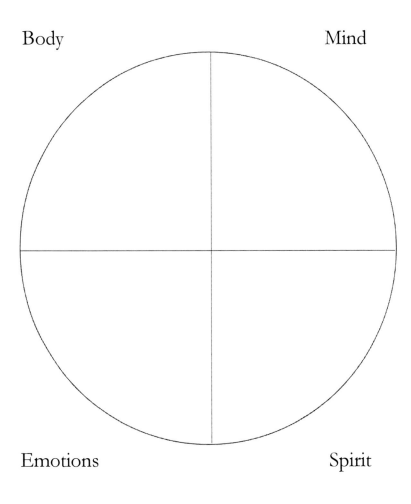

Emotions

Spirit

What have you noticed differently today?

What are you grateful for?

What inspirations have you had today?

Are you doing your Touch/Breath?
- Daily Practice?
- When you get challenged or triggered?

Date:

Body   Mind

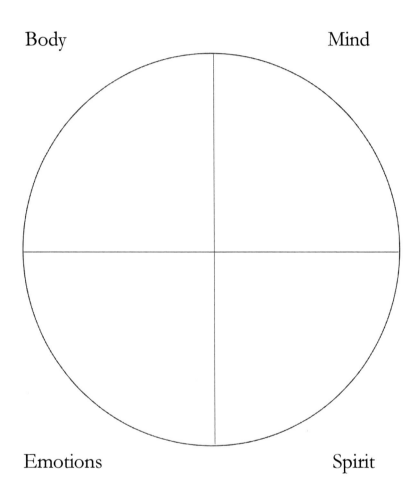

Emotions   Spirit

What have you noticed differently today?

What are you grateful for?

What inspirations have you had today?

Are you doing your Touch/Breath?
- Daily Practice?
- When you get challenged or triggered?

Chapter 8:
Everything is Within Us

Everything is within us. Nassim Haramein's Unified Field Theory physics proves mathematically that each cell is a black hole that contains the entire universe. We have everything we need within us. From this place, says he, we are co-creating our own universe in our perceptual response to the greater potential field of information and collective consciousness.

We are learning, for example, that over 51% of what we see and hear etc. is already programmed in our brain. Our perceptions are mostly controlled by past experiences. How amazing would it be if we were to be clear of these old programs that filter our reality, enabling us to come fresh to each day and each person and each situation with full presence to that moment? This includes both negative and positive programs. If you think about it, how many disappointments have come out of positive expectations projected from the past onto a current or future event? Our conscious and unconscious attachments come from our past programs, both negative and positive. What if we were to be so clear in each moment, that whatever is in front of us, we could respond from our soul's clarity to move us forward in the direction of our individual and collective good; from that place of our individual gifts in service to the whole with compassion and understanding of the innate connection that bonds us in oneness? Truly we are not separate from anything or anyone.

Nassim Haramein's, Bruce Lipton's, Deepak Chopra's, Gregg Braden's, and Lynn McTaggart's science along with many others, now shows us our connectedness and at the same time enlightens us to know that we do not completely create our own realities. We co-create with universal consciousness in a continuous feedback loop. Everything ever thought, done or experienced in our collective consciousness is recorded in the quantum field or vacuum, sometimes referred to as the Akashic Records. We are constantly contributing to this informational field, also known as the Noosphere. With each contributing factor, we alter the collective reality which once again we respond or react to, evolving ourselves through our individual perception and furthering our collectively evolving consciousness. We are individuated points of consciousness, co-creating and co-evolving our universe in a spiral of continuous expression. Now we are conscious of this in greater numbers than ever before, which is speeding up the process and amplifying our collective evolution. Faster, more efficient processes of clearing and connecting to creative solutions are now desperately needed for our survival. Inner Resonance Technologies is an idea whose time is here now.

What is also speeding up the process is that time itself is not what it used to be: Truly. Space and time is curving according to Einstein and as time and space fold and unfold, our realities shift. See Gregg Braden's book "Fractal Time" for further understandings of these principles. Time is 'plastic', just like our brains and our bodies, responding to our timeless minds. Remember Deepak Chopra's early book, "Ageless Body, Timeless Mind"? This material is still relevant and is a great resource for this understanding of the quantum nature of ourselves and our universe.

DNA is now revealed to be a quantum processor. One molecule of DNA was sufficient in 2003 to run the first self-powered nanotechnology computer, the size of a drop of water. Remember, we have approximately 50 trillion cells, according to Dr. Bruce Lipton. That is a WOW! Powerless? I think not: Victim? I think not.

Everything is within us, and it is time to take responsibility for that reality and stop externalizing everything from either a place of blame or supplication to something outside ourselves to save us. We are IT, but we are IT together. What an empowering awareness of freedom that is!

Chapter 9: Conclusion

Empowerment is a side effect of clearing old limiting patterns. Freedom always comes with a corresponding level of responsibility, allowing a new level of choice.

When old patterns are cleared that have kept you stuck, then you are able to respond, as opposed to reacting.

If you are clear, then how you respond becomes a choice. How you respond/react also shows you what is inside YOU: If you are squeezed, what comes out?

Love is a response; frustration, anger and hatred are reactions to unresolved pain inside YOU – WITHOUT EXCEPTION.

At this point you still have a choice: Are you going to 'medicate' from the outside, or heal from the inside?

ARE YOU READY TO TAKE RESPONSIBILITY FOR YOUR OWN TRIGGERS?

Just one touch and breath does it all! That is true empowerment!

Most people who go through this technique clear at such deep, profound levels that 1 to 4 facilitated sessions is all they need. They then carry the tools within to self-clear and create their lives consciously. The 'Speed Dial' or 'Touch/Breath' works better for some than others. A multi-sensory approach is more effective, so whatever the person relates to like a sound or symbol, scent etc. is good. The idea is to have something that is within your own self for an activator. What would happen if you were to lose your 'lucky' rock?

Others (including myself) prefer to have someone facilitate issues once in a while, in between practicing their 'Speed dial', to be able to more fully surrender into a focused intent, especially if a larger issue triggers itself to the surface! We are part of each other and not truly separate so let us help each other.

Remember, we are a 'work in process', never complete on the human level, yet perfectly imperfect on another level which catalyzes our continuous evolution: That is our nature and the nature of our collectively evolving consciousness.

Therefore, there is really no right or wrong or good or bad in this context, only experience and how we choose to respond. I prefer to think of it as what works or doesn't work for you: effective or non-effective.

Once you have internalized tools to take with you, you always have a choice: to use them or not! I speak with some lengthy experience of this myself!

When you are ready to embrace and respond to your journey as a process, surrendering to 'what is' in the context of openness to all possibilities, the irony is that IRT can then take you into unlimited realms of creating new realities in each moment of Now.

If you are committed and ready on any level, there are few techniques available that allow you safer, faster, and more graceful ways to become more of who you are: A miracle creator, effortlessly unleashing your Magical Evolutionary Code, allowing full expression of your true essence with gifts in service to others, moving our greater world into its next octave of creation!

Hopefully, some part of you is ready for the ease of Inner Resonance Technologies, as it is truly an idea whose time is come! Come and play in the Field of Limitless Possibility! All of you are needed to show up! This is where our greatest joy and fulfillment is waiting for us. Your unique self is waiting to be unleashed: Say YES to your Magical Evolutionary Code! Our time is here: We can only succeed together.

In conclusion I would like to share something I wrote for myself eleven years ago and encourage you to do something similar to get clear on your values and your soul's mission. It has been a refresher for my occasionally sagging spirit that once again lifts me up and fills me with inspiration and purpose.

My Personal Vision:

To continue to evolve, express and create more and more from the essence of Love that I AM in all circumstances;

To have command and mastery of my being in greater service for all creation

My Personal Mission/Values/Principles:

By clearing our past programming we have greater freedom to create an improved future in each moment.

I believe we need integrity and personal responsibility to not only clear old, limiting beliefs and patterns but also to empower ourselves and others in expressing and sharing our gifts in service to the Universe.

We all have a special role to play, and it is only by bringing our gifts together that we can create the dream of wholeness.

My Professional Vision:

I would like to make a lasting, impactful contribution to the fields of science and human potential that catalyzes our understanding of ourselves into a new paradigm as unlimited and instant creators in the quantum field of all possibilities.

My Professional Mission:

To create an international, collaborative organization devoted to practicing, teaching and furthering the Inner Resonance Technologies concepts I have developed.

To positively impact all modalities across the spectrum of human endeavour with new possibilities for mankind.

To create the dream together.

This means teaching and learning from each other and supporting each other's weaknesses with our strengths, driven by positive, focused intention.

This means contributing to and celebrating each other's successes as our own.

"With a community of like minds, in a spirit of ego-free collaboration, we are able to weave the strands of our uniqueness into a golden web that supports a balanced, harmonious dance of co-creation!"

Maureen Mason Edwardson

Let me know if you want to dance together!

Our Deepest Fear

Our deepest fear is not that we are inadequate.
Our deepest fear is that we are powerful beyond measure.
It is our light, not our darkness that most frightens us.
We ask ourselves, "Who am I to be brilliant, gorgeous,
Talented and fabulous?"
Actually, who are you not to be?
You are a child of God.
Your playing small doesn't serve the world.
There's nothing enlightened about shrinking so that other
people won't feel insecure around you.
We are all meant to shine, as children do.
We were born to make manifest the glory of
God that is within us.
It's not just in some of us; it's in everyone.
And as we let our own light shine,
We unconsciously give other people permission to do the
same.
As we are liberated from our own fear,
our presence automatically liberates others.

MARIANNE WILLIAMSON
from her book 'A Return To Love'

Resources for More Belief Building

Books

The Biology Of Belief - Unleashing The Power Of Consciousness, Matter And Miracles:

Dr. Bruce Lipton

Spontaneous Evolution - Our Positive Future and How to Get There From Here:

Dr. Bruce Lipton and Steve Bhaerman

The Field - The Quest for the Secret Force of the Universe:

Lynn McTaggart

The Bond - Connecting Through the Space Between Us:

Lynn McTaggart

Instant Healing - Mastering the Way of the Hawaiian Shaman Using Words, Images, Touch, and Energy:

Serge Kahili King

Molecules Of Emotion - The Science Behind Mind-Body Medicine:

Candace Pert PhD

Messages From Water:

Dr Emoto

The Living Energy Universe:

Gary Schwartz & Linda G. Russek

The Cosmic Code - Quantum Physics for the layperson:
Heinz R. Pagels

Conscious Acts of Creation:
William Tiller
The Power of Intention:
Wayne Dyer

Love Without End - Jesus Speaks:
Glenda Green

Science of Getting Rich:
Wallace Wattles

The Genie in Your Genes:
Dawson Church

The God Code:
Gregg Braden

The Divine Matrix:
Gregg Braden

Fractal Time:
Gregg Braden

Ageless Body, Timeless Mind:
Deepak Chopra

Websites

www.brucelipton.com

www.greggbraden.com

www.noetic.org

www.whatthebleep.com

www.theresonanceproject.com

www.barbaramarxhubbard.com

DVDs

Fractal Evolution - The Biology of Consciousness:
Dr. Bruce Lipton (VHS)

Ageless Body Timeless Mind:
Deepak Chopra (VHS)

Messages From Water - Water Crystals in Motion:
Dr. Emoto (DVD)

What the Bleep Do We Know!?:
(DVD/VHS)

Crossing the Event Horizon:
Nassim Haramein (4 DVDs)

The Science of Miracles:

Gregg Braden (DVD)

Biology of Belief Lite:

Dr. Bruce Lipton (DVD)

If you are interested in Inner Resonance workshops or becoming a trainer there are four levels of training:

Introductory Workshop

2.5 hours: morning, afternoon or evening

Level 1: Personal Clearing/ Introduction to Facilitation

For those who want to transform their lives:
2 day Weekend or mid week.
Experiential/ Hands On Training

Level 1: One Day Personal Clearing Intensive: Condensed version of weekend

For those with limited time and resources that want the bones

Level 2: Basic Facilitator Training

Extensive practice with development of personal templates based on Resonance concepts.
For those who want to practice this work with friends and family.
More in-depth scientific understandings 2.5 days

Level 1 – 2 Combo Basic Facilitator

Level 1 – 2 Combo: See descriptions of both levels above which will be offered in combination in a 5 successive day format or over 2 weekends. Combined in immediate succession is recommended for greatest value and effectiveness.

Level 3: Advanced Facilitator Certification (AFC): including integration of other modalities

For those who want to understand the unlimited possibilities of this work and to practice IRT professionally and be able to charge for their sessions.
5 days

Students will be required to document a minimum of 11 sessions before AFC to bring appropriate experiential understandings.

We will go deeper into the scientific background that validates this work. We start by watching the 4 DVDs Crossing the Event Horizon by Nassim Haramein

This is also an introduction to full integration of other modalities. Required reading list includes: Biology of Belief by Dr. Bruce Lipton; The Field by Lynn McTaggart; The Living Energy Universe by Gary Schwartz and Linda Russek. Also recommended is The Genie in My Genes by Dawson Church.

Level 4: Workshop Facilitator Training Program
(Train the Trainer)

For those who want to teach the Basic Practitioner Workshop.

Pre-Requisite Basic Facilitator Training and Advanced Facilitator Certification. A minimum total of 44 documented private sessions is required to demonstrate experience and level of professional intent before the final step of arranging 2 co-teaching workshops:

- As assistant/observer : No Charge
- As full facilitator with myself as assistant : Co-ordinate the event: split proceeds after costs.

- Workshop Facilitators will be certified and registered to deliver the Personal Clearing and the Basic Facilitator Training Levels only and be required to purchase this book as a manual and pay 25% royalties after workshop expenses to the originator Maureen Edwardson.

For more information on Inner Resonance Technologies, workshops, private sessions, speaking engagements and events please go to **www.innerresonance.com** or contact Maureen at **maureen@innerresonance.com**

**Are you an Evolutionary Leader with a message
and interested in becoming an Author of Influence?**

Maureen Edwardson is a graduate of the InspireABook program and a member of the Inspired Authors Circle. If you want to get on the path to be a published author by Influence Publishing please go to **www.InspireABook.com**

For information on the Authors circle and other Authors of Influence please go to **www.InspiredAuthorsCircle.com**

Each month a new book title is released that "Inspires Higher Knowledge" Each pre-launch campaign is supported by the other Authors of Influence with Free E-Books, Audio Books, Mp3's and other gifts. For each book you purchase from the Influence Publishing family you will receive $100's of Free gifts if you support our launches by pre-ordering the books. Take a look at the gifts offered at:
www.SpiritualAuthorsCircle.com/book-launch-gifts/

Influence Publishing

More information on our other titles and how to submit your own proposal can be found at **www.InfluencePublishing.com**

CPSIA information can be obtained at www.ICGtesting.com
Printed in the USA
BVOW03s0208230913

331885BV00010B/74/P